Teaching and Learning
Key Stage 2
Numeracy Activity Book

Subtraction

Hilary Koll
and Steve Mills

EDUCATIONAL

Every effort has been made to trace copyright holders and to obtain their permission for the use of copyright material. The authors and publishers will gladly receive information enabling them to rectify any error or omission in subsequent editions.

First published 1998

Letts Educational, Schools and Colleges Division, 9–15 Aldine Street, London W12 8AW
Tel: 0181 740 2270
Fax: 0181 740 2280

Text © Hilary Koll and Steve Mills
Designed, produced and edited by Gecko Limited,
Bicester, Oxon
Illustrations © Chris Rothero and Mike Parsons

British Library Cataloguing-in-Publication Data
A CIP record for this book is available from the British Library

ISBN 1 84085 112 0
Printed in Great Britain by Ashford Colour Press
Letts Educational is the trading name of BPP [Letts Educational] Ltd

Contents

How to use this book

Mathematics is, for many children, the most difficult subject to learn in school. For many teachers it is a difficult subject to teach well. Why is this? One reason is that mathematics is a hierarchical subject, that is, it's arranged in such a way that certain things need to be understood before much sense can be made of later work. Numbers to 10 need to be understood before we teach numbers to 100, for example.

This is in contrast to most other parts of the primary school curriculum which are less hierarchically arranged. It's possible to know about the Ancient Greeks without knowing anything about the Aztecs, and to understand weather but not settlement. Each one doesn't depend on the other having been understood. Mathematics is not like that, it's like a spy thriller on television with lots of episodes. Miss one and it's difficult to make sense of the rest.

Because of this it is important that we, as teachers of mathematics, have a clear sense of progression within the area of mathematics we are teaching. This helps us to become aware of which episodes children might have missed along the way, and therefore where they are in their understanding. Similarly, it ensures that activities have a clear progression to help children build on to the knowledge and understanding they already have.

This book provides over 60 activities for teaching subtraction and is part of a series of ten books designed to be used in conjunction with the *Teacher's Assessment Book* of this *Key Stage 2 Numeracy Pack*. The *Teacher's Assessment Book* contains **detailed progressions** and **photocopiable diagnostic assessments** for place value, addition, subtraction, multiplication, division, fractions, decimals, percentages, number patterns/algebra and mental mathematics.

The detailed progression and diagnostic test for subtraction will help you to determine the level of children's knowledge and understanding. The test will show where on the subtraction progression children are and, therefore, which of the activities might be most appropriate. The activities are divided into sections which correspond to the statements in the teaching progression for subtraction. Each activity has a specific purpose in relation to this progression. There are activities for *whole-class* use, perhaps as a 10–15-minute introduction, for smaller *group* work and for *individual* work. Each activity has a code which shows how it might be best used.

Summary of codes for the different types of activities/lesson ideas

 This symbol indicates that the activity can be used for whole-class or large-group interactive work. Children will usually be required to sit facing a board or flipchart and the teacher will be expected to lead the discussion/activity. Inclusion of all children in the interactive work will be necessary through questioning and giving examples at a variety of levels for different children. Approximate times are given for these activities.

 This symbol indicates that the activity can be used for group work. This might be an activity on a photocopiable worksheet or one which the teacher introduces verbally to a group. The children can then take this to their 'table' and work cooperatively. There will be times where the teacher is required to support a group in their work and other times when children can work independently. The length of these activities will vary according to the children's abilities.

 This symbol indicates that the activity can be used for individual practice and consolidation work. This might take the form of a photocopiable worksheet or an activity that the teacher can introduce verbally and children can take away to do on their own.

Resources

Most material required for these activities, such as number lines, hundred squares and photocopiable number cards, is included in this book. For many of these activities, however, base 10 material (sometimes called Dienes blocks or hundreds, tens and units) will be required.

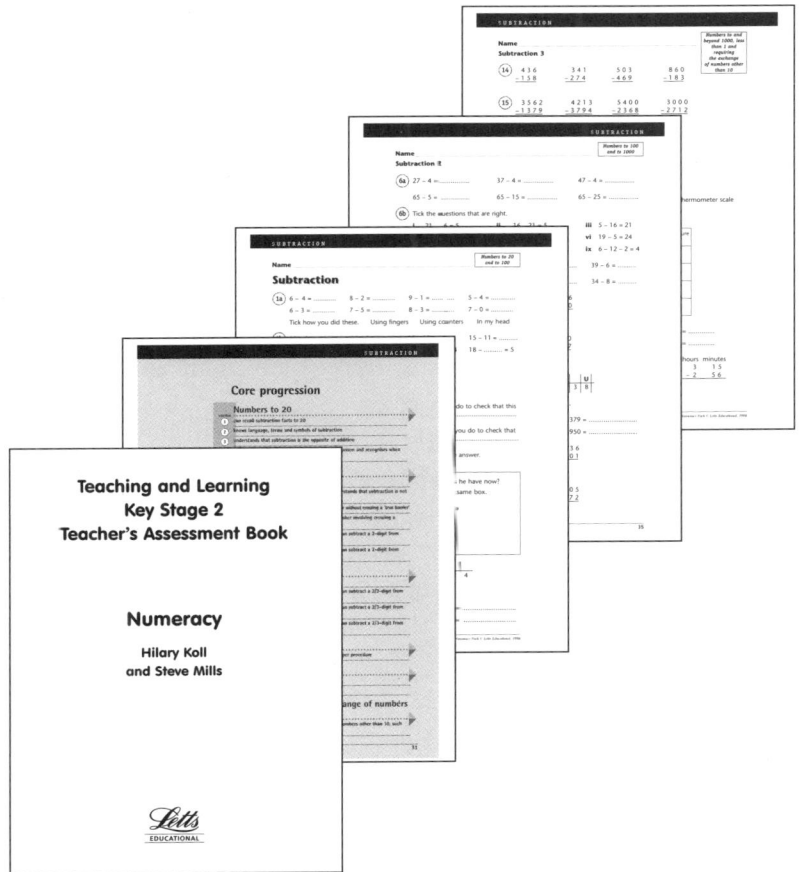

① Can recall subtraction facts to 20

ACTIVITY 1.1

Resources
- two pieces of coloured card

Game show

Two chosen children stand as if in a game show, holding a piece of coloured card as a 'buzzer'. Call out a subtraction question for the children to work out quickly, for example,

'12 minus 7'

As soon as one of the two children knows the answer he/she holds up his/her card and shouts the answer, as if pressing a buzzer. If he/she is correct the opponent is out and another opponent is chosen to face the victor for another round.

Questions should be matched to the two children's abilities, to avoid embarrassment!

ACTIVITY 1.2

Resources
- 'Kate the caterpillar!' sheet on page 7
- counters
- a pack of playing cards

Kate the caterpillar!

A game for 2–4 players.

Children need a copy of Kate the caterpillar each, and enough counters to fit on every segment of her body. The picture cards in the pack can be removed, or used to stand for 10.

Children take turns to take two cards, find the difference and place a counter on that segment of their caterpillar, for example, with the cards 10 and 6:

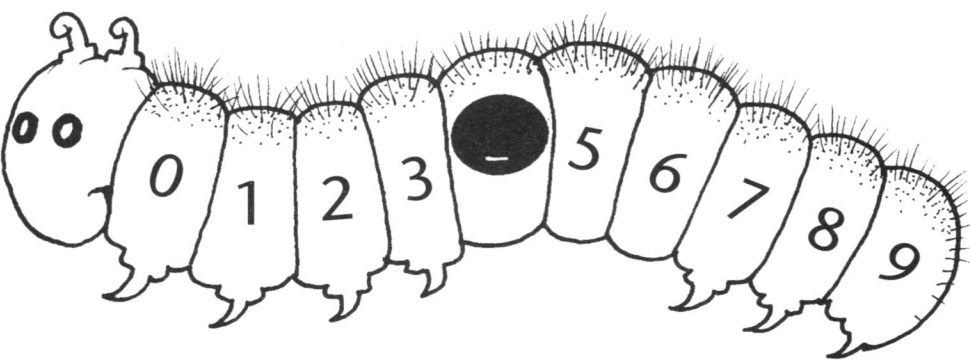

difference = 4

If a counter is already on that section the game moves on to the next player.

The winner is the first player to fill Kate the caterpillar with counters.

ACTIVITY 1.3

Resources
- 'Follow the yellow brick road' sheet on page 8

Follow the yellow brick road

This activity gives children practice at recalling subtraction facts to 20. Try to encourage children to use known facts to work out new facts, for example, using their knowledge that 6 + 6 = 12 to answer 12 – 6 = 6 or 13 – 6 = 7, etc., and to use mental strategies rather than relying on practical methods, for example, using their fingers.

Kate the caterpillar!

You will need a copy of Kate the caterpillar and some counters and a pack of playing cards.

Take it in turns to pick two cards. A picture card stands for 10. Find the difference between the two numbers on your cards, by subtracting the smaller number from the larger number. Put a counter on that section of your caterpillar, unless one is there already. Continue to take it in turns. Watch to check that the other players are getting their subtraction right!

The winner is the player who fills their caterpillar first.

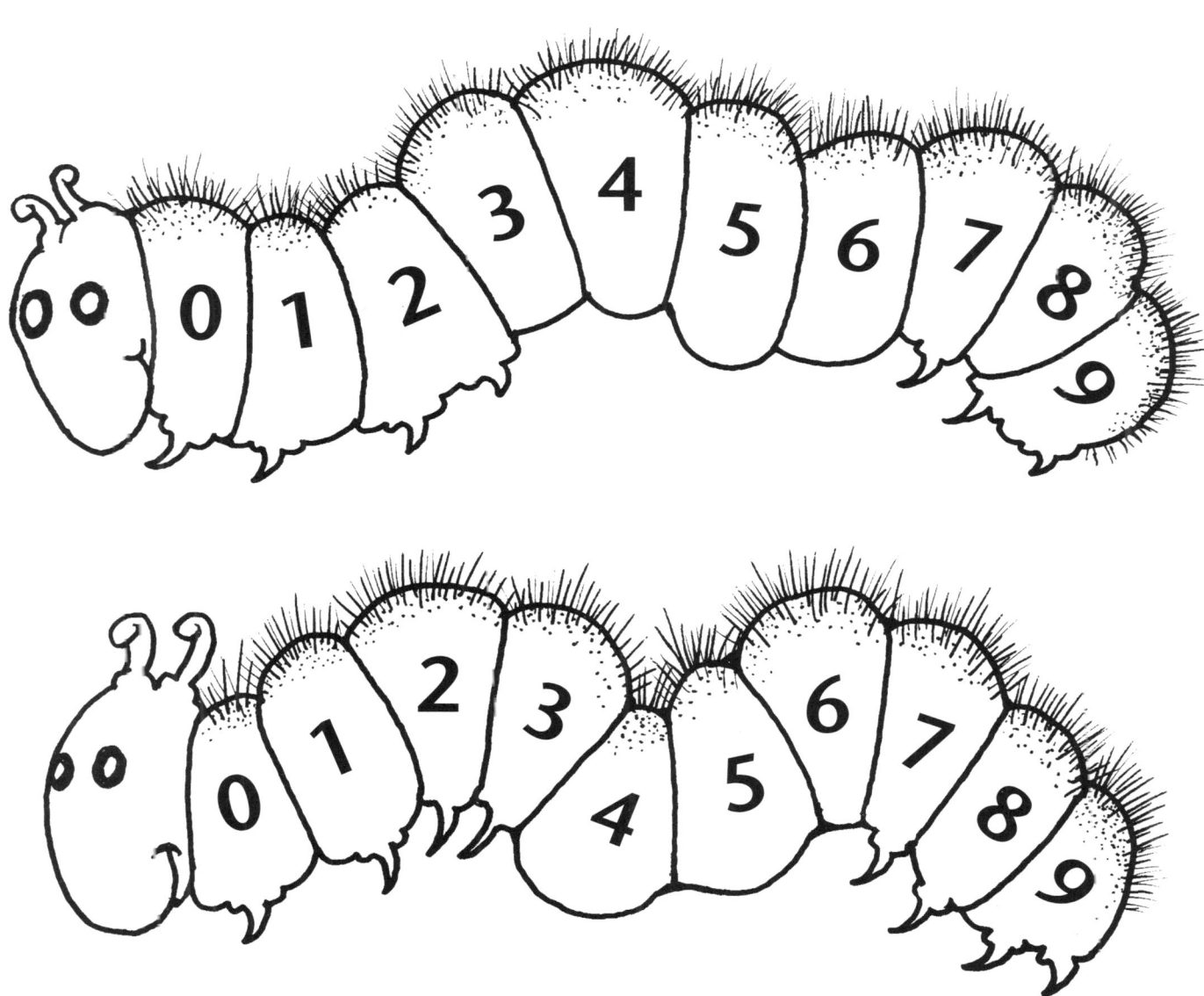

Name ....

Follow the yellow brick road

Answer the questions on the bricks as quickly as you can.

The key at the bottom tells you which bricks should be coloured yellow. Where does the yellow brick road go?

| $17 - 15 =$ | $20 - 10 =$ | $13 - 13 =$ | $16 - 15 =$ | $17 - 13 =$ |

| $8 - 6 =$ | $20 - 13 =$ | $17 - 14 =$ | $17 - 9 =$ | $11 - 9 =$ | $13 - 2 =$ |

| $19 - 11 =$ | $13 - 7 =$ | $16 - 4 =$ | $8 - 6 =$ | $17 - 3 =$ |

| $12 - 11 =$ | $17 - 7 =$ | $15 - 14 =$ | $13 - 6 =$ | $20 - 12 =$ | $14 - 13 =$ |

| $19 - 16 =$ | $12 - 8 =$ | $15 - 8 =$ | $7 - 7 =$ | $12 - 3 =$ |

| $15 - 14 =$ | $14 - 8 =$ | $11 - 1 =$ | $18 - 5 =$ | $17 - 2 =$ | $3 - 2 =$ |

| $18 - 13 =$ | $20 - 11 =$ | $12 - 9 =$ | $14 - 3 =$ | $17 - 8 =$ |

| $15 - 14 =$ | $9 - 7 =$ | $7 - 1 =$ | $6 - 1 =$ | $15 - 4 =$ | $4 - 0 =$ |

| $15 - 11 =$ | $8 - 1 =$ | $14 - 8 =$ | $14 - 11 =$ | $20 - 11 =$ |

| $20 - 9 =$ | $13 - 12 =$ | $16 - 8 =$ | $14 - 7 =$ | $15 - 5 =$ | $18 - 9 =$ |

| $19 - 8 =$ | $16 - 0 =$ | $15 - 10 =$ | $16 - 6 =$ | $12 - 12 =$ |

| $17 - 8 =$ | $13 - 4 =$ | $18 - 12 =$ | $19 - 13 =$ | $12 - 0 =$ | $8 - 6 =$ |

| $12 - 12 =$ | $18 - 8 =$ | $9 - 4 =$ | $9 - 8 =$ | $10 - 5 =$ |

| $6 - 4 =$ | $10 - 0 =$ | $14 - 12 =$ | $8 - 0 =$ | $16 - 5 =$ | $14 - 9 =$ |

Answer to question on brick	Colour of bricks	Answer to question on brick	Colour of bricks	Answer to question on brick	Colour of bricks	Answer to question on brick	Colour of bricks
1	Blue	5	Green	9	Red	13	Green
2	Green	6	Yellow	10	Yellow	14	Red
3	Yellow	7	Red	11	White	15	White
4	Red	8	Blue	12	Blue	16	Blue
						0	White

(2) Knows language, terms and symbols of subtraction

ACTIVITY 2.1

Resources
- none

The meaning game

On the board draw two large rectangles as shown below. In the first rectangle write the word 'Happy' and ask the children to suggest words that mean the same as happy. Encourage the children to think of as many words as they can. Explain to the children that different words can mean the same thing.

Happy	Subtraction

In the second rectangle write the word 'Subtraction', ask the children what it means and write class definitions on the board.

Encourage children now to offer alternative words or phrases for subtraction and record them in the second box on the board. At this point you have the opportunity to become aware of any misconceptions of the term 'subtraction' and can rectify the situation during the following mathematics sessions. If the children have difficulty with alternative words, then you can take a more leading role in the discussion by offering words to the children. These could include:

minus, subtract, take away, less, take, difference between, less than

Children can be encouraged to make up subtraction questions using these different words, for example, 'If I had 4 red pens and James had 3 fewer, how many did James have?' 'What is the difference between 7 and 12?'

If the class is given one question, such as 14 – 5 = 9, each child can invent a different story, and these can be discussed and recorded as a whole group, pointing out any use of the above words.

ACTIVITY 2.2

Resources
- 'The answer is...' sheet on page 11

The answer is...

This activity can help children to become familiar with the terms and symbols related to subtraction. It also provides practice in recalling subtraction facts to 20 and, in particular, those related to the numbers 7 and 8. Children tend not to learn these facts as quickly as others. Try to encourage children to use known facts to work out new facts, for example, using their knowledge that 6 + 6 = 12 to answer 12 – 6 = 6 or 13 – 6 = 7, etc., and to use mental strategies rather than relying on practical methods, for example, using their fingers.

ACTIVITY

2.3

Resources
■ none

Stories with a difference

Give children a number of questions, for example, 15 – 4, 16 – 13, etc. Ask them to create stories around each question which involve words associated with subtraction, for example, 'I had 15 counters and lost 4'.

Extension work can involve children in creating questions rather than statements, for example, 'Jane had 10 sweets. Julie had 15. How many more did Julie have than Jane?'

ACTIVITY

2.4

Resources
■ cards made from resource sheet 1 on page 58

Going loopy!

A game for 4–6 players.

Children need to share out the cards.

Player 1 lays a card down on the table and reads the question at the bottom, for example,

13

18 minus 6

The player who has the card marked 12 (the answer to '18 minus 6') then places this card on top of it, and reads out the question at the bottom, for example,

12

15 take away 5

The player with the card marked 10 places it on top and so on.

The game continues until all the cards have been placed on the table.

The winner is the player who lays down all his/her cards first.

The answer is...

7   or   8

Draw two columns into your book. Write 7 at the top of one column and 8 at the top of the other. Write out all the following questions in their correct columns.

$14 - 7 =$ the difference between 2 and 10 is ...

$15 - 2 - 2 - 3 =$ seven take away zero is ....

subtract 4 from 11 = $15 - 8 =$

16 minus 8 is ....   3 less than 10 is ....

$13 - 2 - 2 - 1 =$ the difference between 15 and 8 is ......

19 subtract 12 is ....   18 minus ...... is 10

9 is .... less than 17   .... minus 8 is 0

18 take away 11 = $12 - 4 =$

19 minus 12 =   how many more is 13 than 5?

$17 - 3 - 3 - 3 =$ the difference between 12 and 5 is ...

$13 - .... = 5$ 12 less than 19 is ....

subtract 6 from 13 $11 - 3 =$

$12 - 5 =$ 16 take 9 is ....

eight less than sixteen is ....   14 subtract 6 is ......

Make up some questions of your own where the answers are 7 or 8.

③ Understands that subtraction is the opposite of addition

ACTIVITY 3.1

Resources
- resource sheet 4: 0–100 number line on page 61
- small piece of card in the shape of a frog
- blu-tack to stick frog to number line

Leap frog

Draw or put on display a 0–20 number line, like the one below.

Explain to the children that Freddy the Frog hops up and down this path. Sometimes he makes big jumps, at other times small jumps. We can write down his moves like this.

From 0 jumping forwards 2   we can write as $0 + 2 = 2$
From 2 jumping forwards 3   we can write as $2 + 3 = 5$

Show Freddy making the moves. A piece of cardboard shaped like a frog with blu-tack stuck on the reverse side is useful for this. Remind the children that we do **not** count the number Freddy is standing on as part of the move.

Encourage children to come up to the board and write the sum, or to demonstrate where Freddy would move to, from a given sum.
Use addition only at this stage.

Begin again on 0 and give the children the sum $0 + 5 = 5$. Ask a child to show this move. Ask 'If Freddy wanted to go back to 0, how many would he have to jump?' 'How could we write this move?'

Encourage children to use the subtraction sign to write $5 - 5 = 0$.

Again, give children moves backwards from larger numbers, for example, from 10 jumping backwards 6, and ask them to write these moves as subtraction questions, for example, $10 - 6 = 4$. Alternatively, provide them with subtraction questions and ask them to demonstrate Freddy's movements.

ACTIVITY 3.2

Resources
- none

Chains

Draw this chain on the board, as shown.

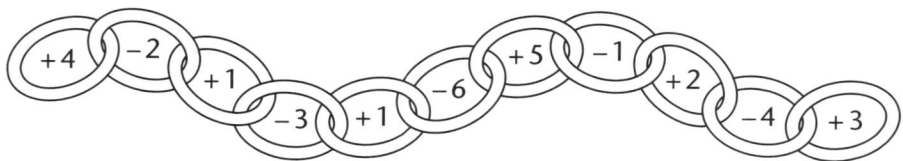

Choose a number above 5 and ask the children to follow the chain. Ask them 'What number do you finish with?' 'What do you notice?' 'Does it always work?' Choose another number above 5 and try again.

Begin from the other end and go backwards. Ask 'Does it still work?' 'Why does it work?'

If you group all the addition links together and add them they equal the number that all the subtraction links make. Remind the children that addition and subtraction are opposite.

A follow-up activity can involve children making up their own chains, like this, which end and begin on the same number.

Resources
■ resource sheet
4: 0–100
number line
on page 61
is useful

Rosie and Jim

Draw the following function machine people on the board, as shown below.

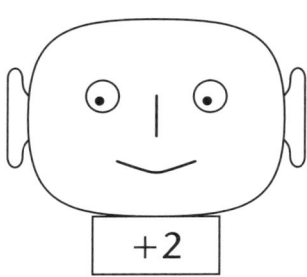

Begin with the smiling girl on the left. This is Rosie. Explain that Rosie is a good girl who likes to be helpful and always does what she is told.

Write +2 in the box underneath her. Whatever numbers she is given, she will always add 2 to them. Write some 'input' numbers on her left, for example,

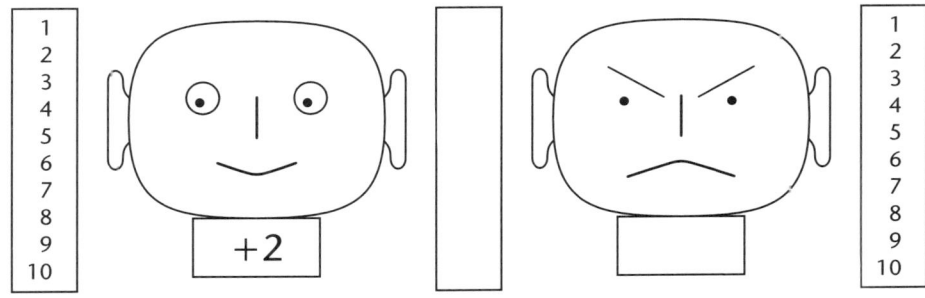

Encourage the children to come up to the board and write the 'output' numbers on her right. Discuss what has happened to the numbers. A 0–20 number line can be used to show how the numbers have moved along 2 places.

Give Rosie a new 'function', for example, +4. Using the same input numbers, find her output numbers. Ensure that the children have understood that the same thing happens to each number.

Rosie can be given a new set of output numbers, for example, 6, 7, 8, 9 and the children can be asked to find 'the rule', for example, +5.

When children appear to be confident with this process, introduce Jim. Jim is a mischievous boy, who always tries to undo anything that Rosie does.

If Rosie has added 2 to each number, Jim will try to undo it, so that we return to the numbers started with. What will Jim do? (–2)

Give children rules for Rosie and go through finding output numbers. What will Jim need to do to return to the original numbers?

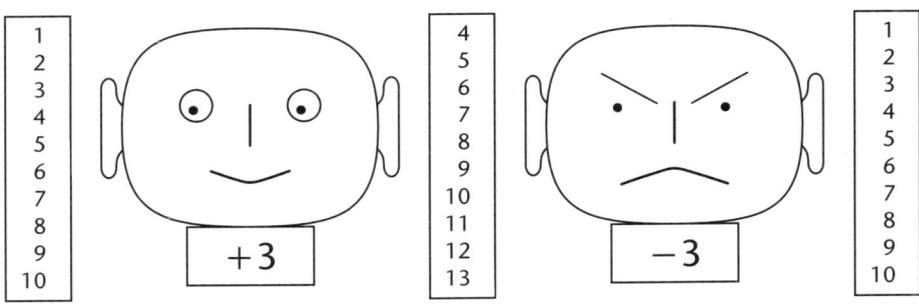

Resources
- a dice
- 'Football fever' sheet on page 15 or resource sheet 4: 0–100 number line on page 61, if preferred
- a counter can be used instead of the football players and ball

Football fever

A game for 2 players.

Children begin by putting the ball on the centre spot of the football pitch. One player 'adds' at all times, the other player 'subtracts'. They take it in turns to roll the dice and move the ball that number in either direction. Encourage the children to say their move, for example, '10 take away 4 is 6'. Whoever reaches their goal scores.

You can also ask the children to record their moves as a chain or a string of operations, for example, $10 - 2 + 4 - 6 + 1 - 5 + 1 - 3 = 0$ Goal!!!

These chains can then be used for mental mathematics practice, to be given orally, with a few seconds allowed between each operation.

Resources
- none

Making a statement

Draw a chart on the board, like the one shown below.

Day	Pay in	Take out	Amount

Explain that this is someone's bank statement, showing how many pounds they put in and how many pounds they take out, over one week.

Fill in the chart like this.

Day	Pay in	Take out	Amount
Monday	£10		£10

Explain what this shows, before continuing.

Day	Pay in	Take out	Amount
Monday	£10		£10
Tuesday	£5		£.....

Encourage the children to come up to the board and write in the amount at the end of each day. Continue the chart for a week. Ask 'Is there more money in the account at the end of the week than after the first day?' 'What are we doing to the numbers if we pay in some money?' (adding) 'What are we doing to the numbers as we take money out?' (subtracting). Show the children how a process can be reversed, for example, paying in £5 (+5) can be reversed by taking out £5 (–5). Addition is the opposite (inverse) of subtraction and vice versa.

You can use Activity 3.6 'Save, spend, save' on page 16 to consolidate this idea.

Resources
- 'Save, spend, save' sheet on page 16

Save, spend, save

This activity follows Activity 3.5 'Making a statement' and gives children a real context to explore addition and subtraction as inverses. They are required to calculate the weekly balance in a bank account by adding or subtracting amounts of money.

Questions are then asked about the account, encouraging children to observe more closely the effect of addition followed by subtraction, in order to develop a fuller awareness of subtraction and addition as inverses.

Football fever

A game for 2 players.

You will need a dice and a ball, like this one. Cut out this ball or make one of your own.

Start by putting the ball on the centre spot of the football pitch. Take it in turns to roll the dice and move the ball that number in your direction. One player moves towards one goal, adding each time; the other player moves towards the other goal, taking away. Whoever reaches their goal scores and you return to the centre spot to try again. The winner is the player who has scored most goals in the time allowed.

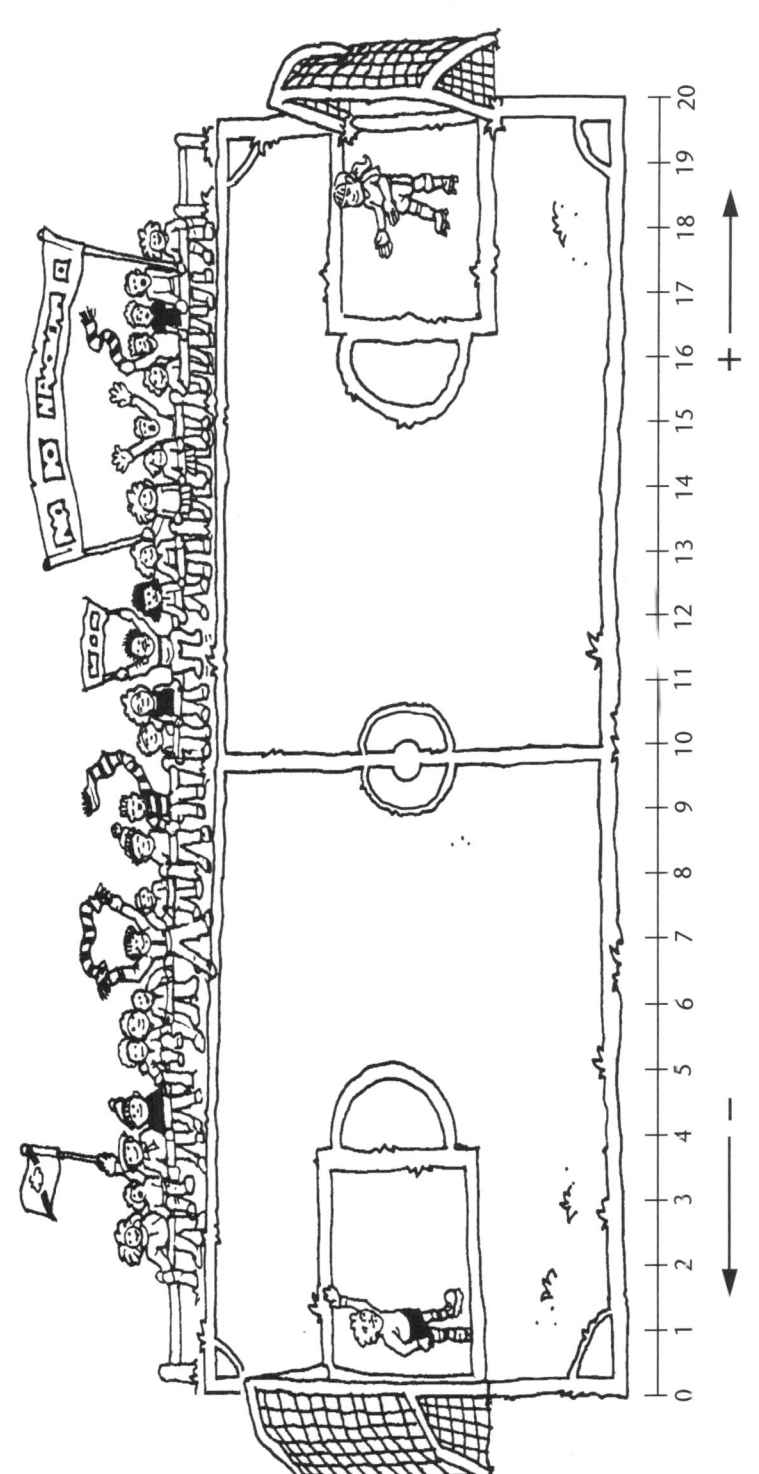

Name ....

Save, spend, save

Here is Alison's bank statement. She earns money each week from doing jobs for her friends and family. Sometimes she spends her money and sometimes she saves it. She has a bank account where she puts money she wants to save. Fill in the end column to show how much money is in her account (the account balance).

Date	Money paid in	Money taken out	Account balance
1 Jan	£15		£15
12 Jan		£4	
27 Jan	£2		
15 Mar		£6	
20 Mar	£12		
6 Apr		£12	
20 Jun	£8		
11 Jul	£3		
21 Aug		£3	
7 Sept		£4	
14 Sept		£5	
2 Oct	£5		
17 Oct		£1	
5 Nov	£10		
9 Dec		£20	
25 Dec	£4		

When did Alison have the most money in her account? ....

When did she have the least money? ....

KS2 Numeracy Pack © Letts Educational, 1998

④ Understands subtraction as taking away and comparison and recognises when subtraction is necessary

ACTIVITY

4.1

Resources
- none

What's the difference?

This activity demonstrates subtraction as comparison. Draw a simple number line going up from zero vertically, like the one below.

Draw two stick dolls of different heights, their feet level with zero, on the board and ask 'What is the difference in their heights?'. Explain that the answer to this requires more than just a description. In mathematics we expect a number for the answer. How can we find the difference?

Show how we look at the height of both dolls to see how many more units one is than the other.

Draw more dolls and encourage the children to come up to the board and explain how they worked out the answer. Methods can include: counting on from the smaller number, counting back from the larger, subtracting the smaller from the larger, using addition saying, for example, $7 + ? = 10$, and so on. Continue to ask the question 'What is the difference...' for this activity.

You can use Activity 4.3 'Goal differences' on page 19 to consolidate this idea.

Resources
- a collection of 20 objects, such as conkers, bears, counters or cubes
- piece of paper for recording

Take it away

A game for 2–3 players.

This game reinforces the idea of subtraction as 'taking away' rather than comparison. Children will need a collection of 20 items/counters/cubes in the middle of the table and a piece of paper per group for recording. They begin by counting the objects together to check that there are 20.

Each player takes it in turns to take away either 1, 2, or 3 items from the pile and discard them to one side. The number of each 'take-away' and the number of objects left should be recorded, for example,

$$
\begin{array}{ll}
20 & -3 \\
17 & -2 \\
15 & -1 \ \text{etc.}
\end{array}
$$

Players continue taking away 1, 2, or 3, whichever they choose. The winner is the player who removes the last remaining object or objects; that is, the player who must perform the final subtraction to reach zero.

As children repeat this activity, encourage them to recall the number of objects remaining, rather than having to count them. You should also encourage them to look for strategies for winning, i.e. if there are two players and one makes a subtraction leaving four objects on the table, that player will win.

Resources
- 'Goal differences' sheet on page 19
- current football league tables will be useful

Goal differences

In this activity, children are asked to calculate the goal differences of a number of football teams. The goal difference of a particular team is the difference between the number of goals the team has scored and the number of goals the team has let in.

The best goal difference is the largest difference.

Current football league tables can be used, although negative numbers can occur when teams have let in more goals than they have scored.

Resources
- 'Difference search' sheet on page 20
- coloured pencils

Difference search

In this activity, children begin by writing pairs of numbers with a difference of 5, using numbers up to 20. They then find these pairs of numbers in the grid and draw a ring around them using red pencil. Number pairs must be next to each other either vertically, diagonally or horizontally. Children then repeat this for numbers with a difference of 7. This sheet can be adapted for other differences, or children can make up their own grids.

Name ....

Goal differences

To find the goal difference we take the number of goals scored by a team and subtract the goals scored against them. Fill in this table to find out which team has the best goal difference.

Team	Goals scored	Goals against	Goal difference
Arsenal	9	5	
Manchester United	10	3	
Liverpool	8	6	
Spurs	7	4	
Newcastle	9	6	
Chelsea	8	2	
Blackburn	7	1	

Which team has the best goal difference? ....

Find some current football tables from a newspaper. Which team has the best goal difference? Fill in this table.

Team	Goal difference

Name ....

Difference search

Write down some pairs of numbers that have a difference of 5, for example,

9 – 4   8 – 3   19 – 14

Use numbers up to 20. See if you can find more than 10 pairs of numbers.

Look at the numbers in this grid.

Using a red pencil, draw a ring around numbers next to each other that have a difference of 5.

One has been done for you.

5	7	19	4	0	9	5	9
2	8	0	8	3	12	5	7
10	0	9	3	6	15	4	3
6	7	20	1	11	3	5	1
8	4	1	18	5	4	9	4
2	5	10	8	0	6	13	10
15	6	5	13	3	13	18	8
6	3	16	8	9	10	11	0
5	17	12	4	12	5	9	7
9	6	12	2	4	1	4	1

On the same grid, look for any numbers next to each other that have a difference of 7. Use a green pencil to draw a circle around these.

Make up a grid of your own to find other differences.

KS2 Numeracy Pack © Letts Educational, 1998

⑤ Understands place value ideas to 100

Further activities can be found in the Place Value Teaching and Learning Activity Book *in this series.*

ACTIVITY 5.1

Resources
■ none

Gritty grids

Draw a 4×4 grid. Put in any numbers from 1 to 100 randomly.

For example,

26	56	62	15
13	32	18	78
99	82	12	68
40	7	91	32

This grid can be used for asking questions such as the following.

'How many numbers can you see that have 2 units?'
'Which numbers are between 10 and 20?'
'Which numbers are made from 4 tens?'
'Which numbers have the same number of tens as units?'

Find a route from side to side, or top to bottom, where the units digits are less than 3.

Find a route where the tens digits are less than 4.

Encourage children to partition the numbers into their tens and units parts, for example, 78 = 70 + 8 or 7 tens and 8 units, etc.

ACTIVITY 5.2

Resources
■ none

Doing the splits

Write this number chain on the board, or a similar one which follows the same pattern where either the tens or the units digit stays the same.

27   37   35   45   35   39   29   27   26   86   82   92   91

Ask the children if they can see a pattern.

Begin with the first number. Split it up for children to see, for example,

$$27 = 20 + 7.$$

Then ask them how the next number can be made. Write this underneath the previous partitioning, for example,

$$27 = 20 + 7$$
$$37 = 30 + 7$$

Ask them what they notice.

Continue the process until the end of the numbers. Encourage children to come up and write the partitioning on the board.

Resources
- 'Partition party' sheet on page 23

Partition party

This activity provides children with practice in splitting and rejoining numbers, using tens and units. It draws children's attention to the differences between the tens and units digits and encourages them to appreciate that the position of a digit signifies its value.

Resources
- calculators

Disappearing heroes

Ask children to type a 2-digit number into the calculator. They have to make each of the digits disappear, leaving an empty space or a zero. They must do this by subtracting an amount. If they have been introduced to the Superheroes idea in the *Place Value Teaching and Learning Activity Book* in this series, encourage them to talk of the tens digit, for example, as 'I'm going to make Tens Man disappear!'.

For example, if our number is 53, we must subtract 50 in order to remove the tens digit.

$$53 - 50 = 3$$

This activity helps children to focus on the value of each digit as determined by its position in a number.

Ask children to discuss what needs to be subtracted to remove each digit in turn. At first, children may make mistakes, for example, to remove Tens Man in the number 53 children may subtract 5, rather than 50.

If mistakes are made, ask them to try adding the number they subtracted to return to the original number.

Further explanation of the Superheroes can be found in Unit 13 (pages 43–45) of this book.

Resources
- one calculator per child

Moving targets

A game for 2 players.

Player 1 enters a 2-digit number into his calculator, for example, 47. Player 2 enters the same number into her calculator but with 1 digit changed, for example, 43 or 97. Player 1 must change his display to match that of player 2 in one operation, as in adding 50 if the new number is 97.

If player 1 is correct, he scores 1 point. Then player 2 selects a number and the game continues.

The winner is the first player to score 11 points.

This activity helps children to focus on the value of each digit as determined by its position in a number.

Name ....

Partition party

Partitioning is when we split numbers up into parts, like this.

$$\boxed{4 \mid 1} = \boxed{4 \; 0} + \boxed{1}$$

Write these in the same way.

52	**84**	**45**
11	**92**	**71**
94	**29**	**79**
55	**41**	**12**
19	**25**	**49**

Rejoin these numbers that have been partitioned.

40 + 2 = ...   30 + 7 = ...   70 + 4 = ...

80 + 8 = ...   10 + 9 = ...   40 + 6 = ...

90 + 4 = ...   40 + 1 = ...   10 + 1 = ...

20 + 7 = ...   60 + 0 = ...   90 + 8 = ...

70 + 0 = ...   0 + 8 = ...   20 + 2 = ...

30 + 5 = ...   80 + 3 = ...   30 + 1 = ...

Make up some more of your own.

⑥ Can see patterns within numbers to 100 and understands that subtraction is not commutative or associative

ACTIVITY 6.1

Resources
- resource sheet 4: 0–100 number line on page 61 or 100 square is useful

What difference does it make?

Write the following 2-digit numbers on the board, as shown.

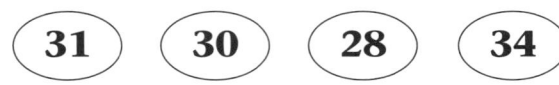

Ask the children to put the numbers in order, smallest first.

Explain that you are going to choose two of the numbers and to find the difference. (Alternatively, you could say you are taking the smaller number from the larger number.)

Write this difference on the board, like this.

$$\bigcirc - \bigcirc = 4$$

Which of the two numbers could it be? When children give the answer, ask them what they looked for.

Give some more differences, for example,

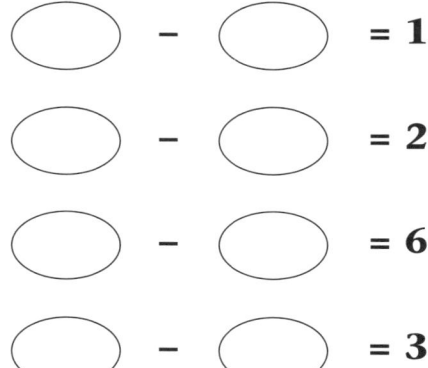

Note there are two answers to the difference of 3.

Underneath the original numbers write four more 2-digit numbers, with similar units digits, for example,

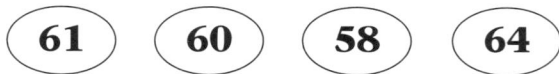

and ask the children to work out the differences. Do they notice that the differences are the same as in the previous example? Use a number line or 100 square to show them that the numbers are just repeated further along the line. Encourage them to describe patterns they can see and discuss the strategies they use for calculating difference.

The activity can be repeated many times with different 2-digit numbers.

Resources
- base 10 material
- resource sheet 4: 0–100 number line on page 61 is useful

Take patterns

Write the following subtraction question on the board. Ask two children to come up to the board and stand in front of it to collect the correct number of tens and units, using the base 10 material. One child should hold the ten sticks, the other the unit cubes, for example,

28 – 5

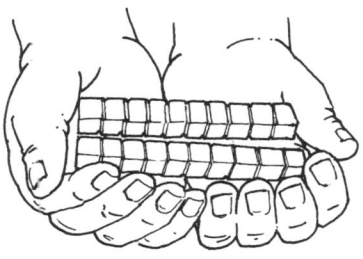

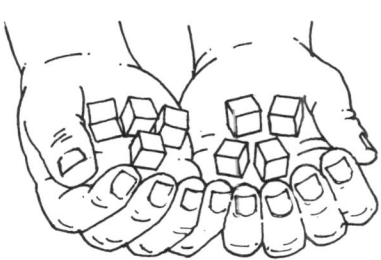

2 tens   8 units

Proceed with the subtraction, taking away 5 units. Draw children's attention to the child holding the tens sticks. Did he/she have to do anything?

Write on the board:

48 – 5

Demonstrate this again, using the children and the base 10 material.

Repeat for the following:

58 – 5   98 – 5 etc.

until all the children have recognised the pattern. For these examples, the children need to know 8 – 5 = 3.

Encourage the children to see that patterns repeat themselves as numbers are increased by ten each time. Without using materials, can they answer 57 – 2 or 79 – 6?

When children are confident with numbers that do not require exchange or the crossing of a 'tens barrier', this activity can be repeated with questions like 43 – 7. Draw their attention to the fact that, in this case, the child holding the tens will be involved.

Resources
- none

Take investigations

This investigation can assist children to see that patterns repeat themselves as numbers are increased by ten.

Ask children, in groups, to explore all the possible solutions to the following question.

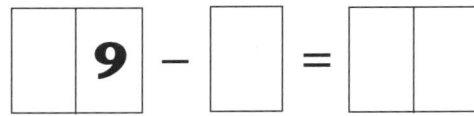

Children will discover that all the numbers from 0 to 99 can be made. Encourage the groups to present their information in a poster form and systematically to ensure that questions for all the solutions are found.

You can adapt this investigation by giving the children a particular single-digit number to subtract or by changing the units digit so that the subtraction may require the crossing of a 'tens barrier'.

(7) Can mentally subtract a 1-digit from a 2-digit number without crossing a 'tens barrier'

ACTIVITY 7.1

Resources
- resource sheet 4: 0–100 number line on page 61 is useful

Pretty patterns

Draw two similar snakes on the board, as shown below.

Choose a single-digit number above 3 and write it into the first segment of the top snake. Ask the children to add 10 to the number and write that number in the next segment. Continue adding ten and writing the new number in the neighbouring segment until the snake is filled.

Write **–4** underneath the snake and ask the children to subtract 4 from the first number. Write this answer into the first segment of the second snake, for example,

Continue to subtract 4 from each of the numbers in the top snake. What do the children notice about the numbers? Why does this happen? Use a number line to demonstrate that numbers to 100 follow similar patterns, going up in tens.

Repeat this activity, beginning with a different single-digit number and a new number to subtract.

ACTIVITY 7.2

Resources
- 'Avoid the sharks!' sheet on page 27
- dice
- counters

Avoid the sharks!

A game for 2 players. Each player needs an 'Avoid the sharks!' sheet.

The first player begins by selecting a number from the box at the top of the sheet, then rolls the dice, and subtracts the number rolled on the dice from the larger number. If the answer is on the sheet then a counter is placed on this number. The players take turns to choose a number from the box at the top of the sheet and to subtract from it the number rolled on the dice.

The winner is the first player to cover all the circled numbers on the sheet to reach the other side of the river.

ACTIVITY 7.3

Resources
- 'Wagon wheels' sheet on page 28

Wagon wheels

This activity gives children the opportunity to practise subtracting a single digit from a 2-digit number without crossing a 'tens barrier'.

Avoid the sharks!

A game for 2 players.

You will need a dice and some counters for this game.

Take it in turns to choose a number from the box below. Roll the dice and take the number on the dice away from the number you have chosen. If the answer is in one of the circles below, put a counter on it. If not, the other player has a turn.

The winner is the player to cover all the circled numbers and reach the other side of the river.

| 38 | 67 | 36 | 47 | 66 | 48 | 97 | 69 | 29 | 96 |

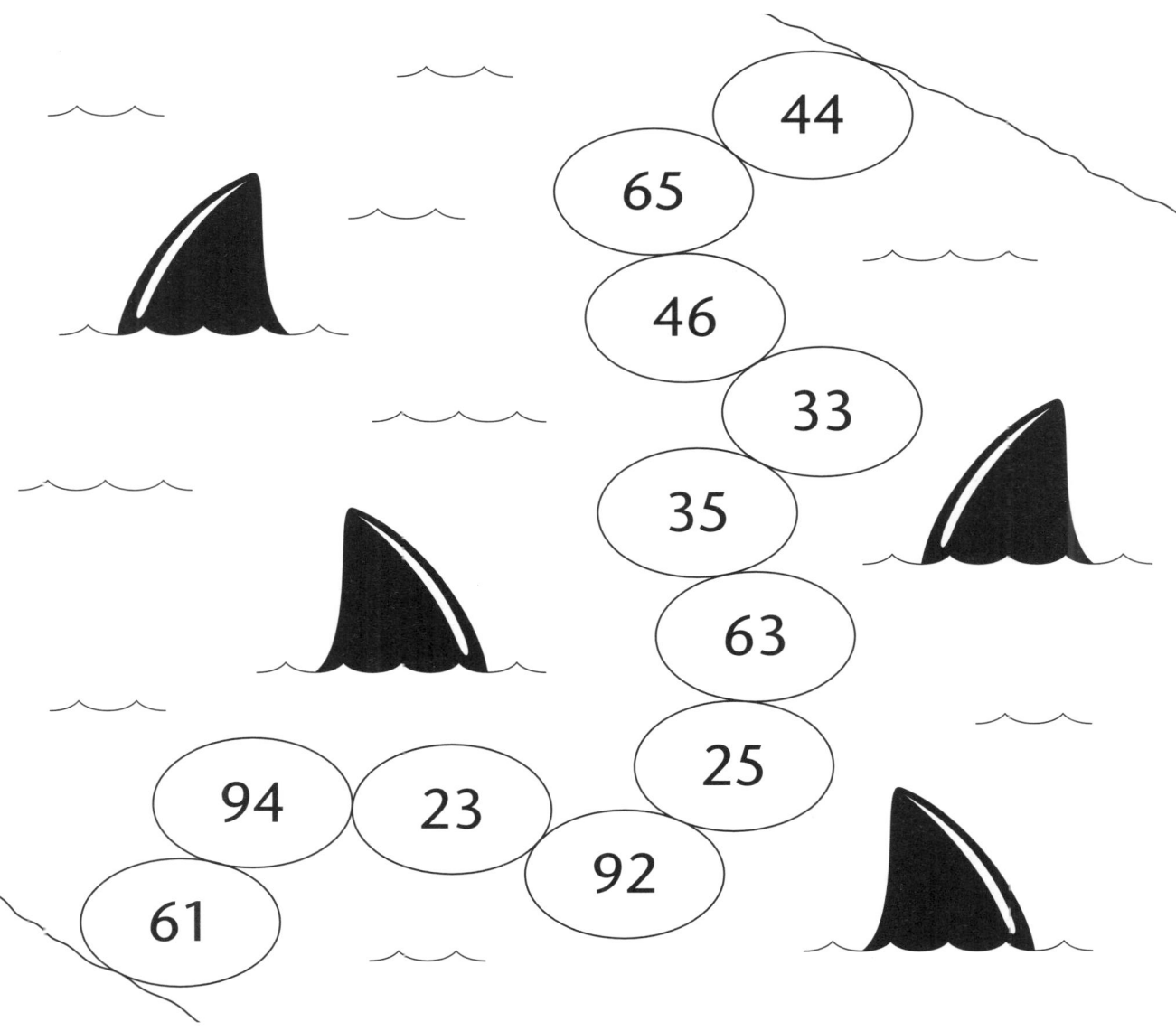

7.3

Name

Wagon wheels

Fill in the numbers at the end of the spokes. How quickly can you finish each wheel?

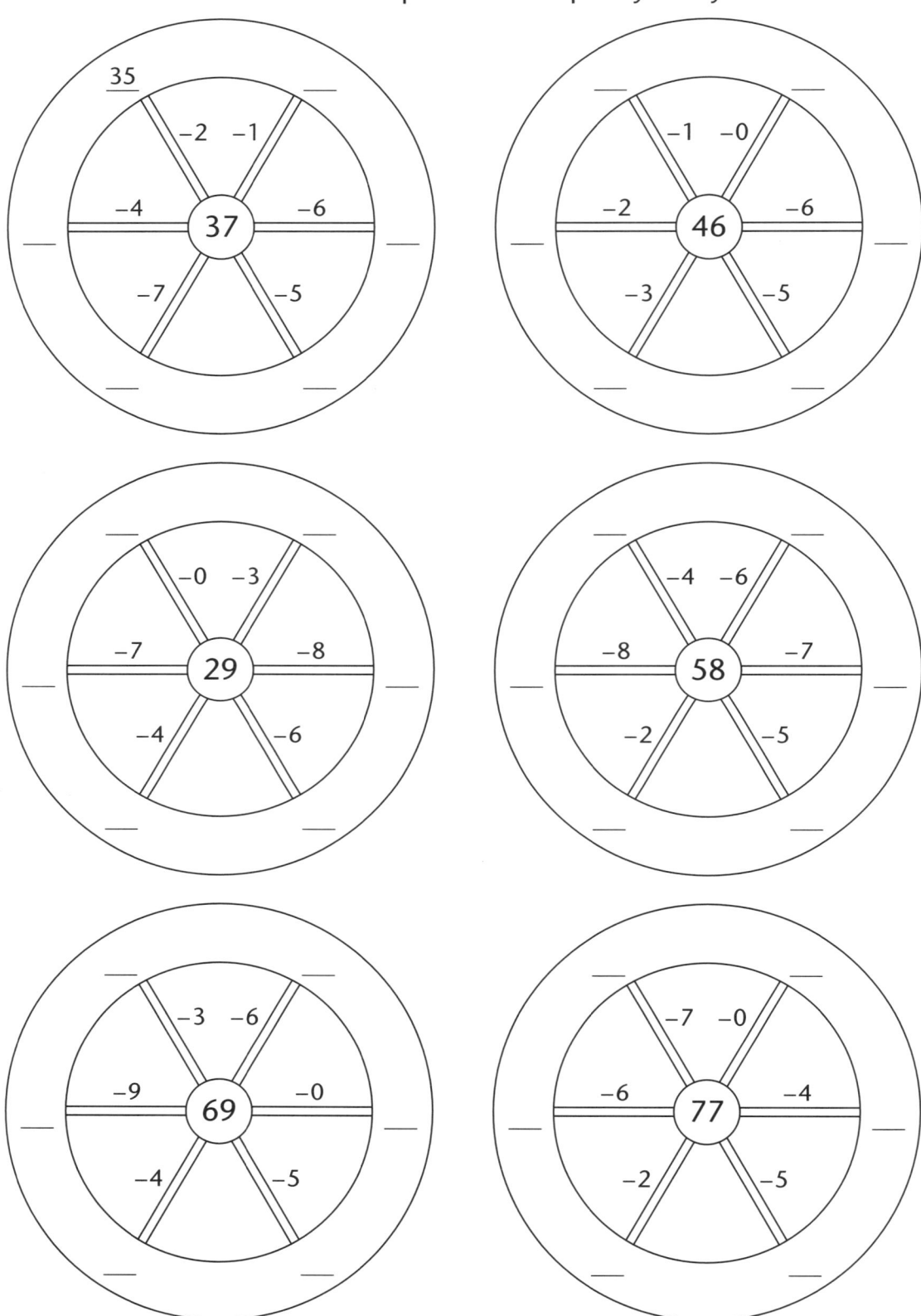

Draw some more wheels of your own. Ask your friends to try to fill in the numbers.

(8) Can mentally subtract a 1-digit from a 2-digit number involving crossing a 'tens barrier'

ACTIVITY 8.1

Resources
- pack of cards

A dart to the heart

This game can be played with the whole class, splitting the children into groups.

It is based on the game of darts, but instead of stepping up and throwing a dart, the players from each team step up and choose a card from the pack (picture cards removed). Each team begins with a score of 99 and as a card is selected, this is subtracted from their score. You can record the running totals on the board for all teams to see. The winning team is the team who lands on exactly zero. If a card is selected which would take the score below zero, it is ignored and play passes to the next team.

The game can be played by small groups, as outlined in Activity 8.2 *'Darts clubs'* below.

ACTIVITY 8.2

Resources
- pack of cards
- piece of paper for recording

Darts clubs

This is a game for 2–4 players. The game is outlined above in Activity 8.1 *'A dart to the heart'*, but here it is played as individuals. Children will need an introduction to this game and should be encouraged to record their own scores on paper.

ACTIVITY 8.3

Resources
- 'Zero hero' sheet on page 30
- a counter or a coin

Zero hero

A game for 2 players.

The players agree on a start number between 50 and 100. They then take turns to place the coin or counter on a circle and subtract the number above it from the running total. The winner is the player who finally subtracts to leave the total at exactly zero. A player who scores lower than zero loses.

ACTIVITY 8.4

Resources
- 'Pick a path' sheet on page 31

Pick a path

This activity gives children the opportunity for 2-digit minus 1-digit subtraction in the context of spending money as they move through a grid. The aim is to plot paths which allow the money remaining from £1 to match an amount on the 'Finish line'.

Zero hero

A game for 2 players.

You will need a counter or a coin.

Choose a start number between 50 and 100. Put the counter or coin on one of the circles next to the numbers in the grid. Take that number away from the start number. The next player moves the counter or coin to another circle and takes that number away from the new number. Keep taking turns to move the counter or coin and subtract. The winner is the player who makes the total to equal zero.

If you make the number less than zero, you lose!

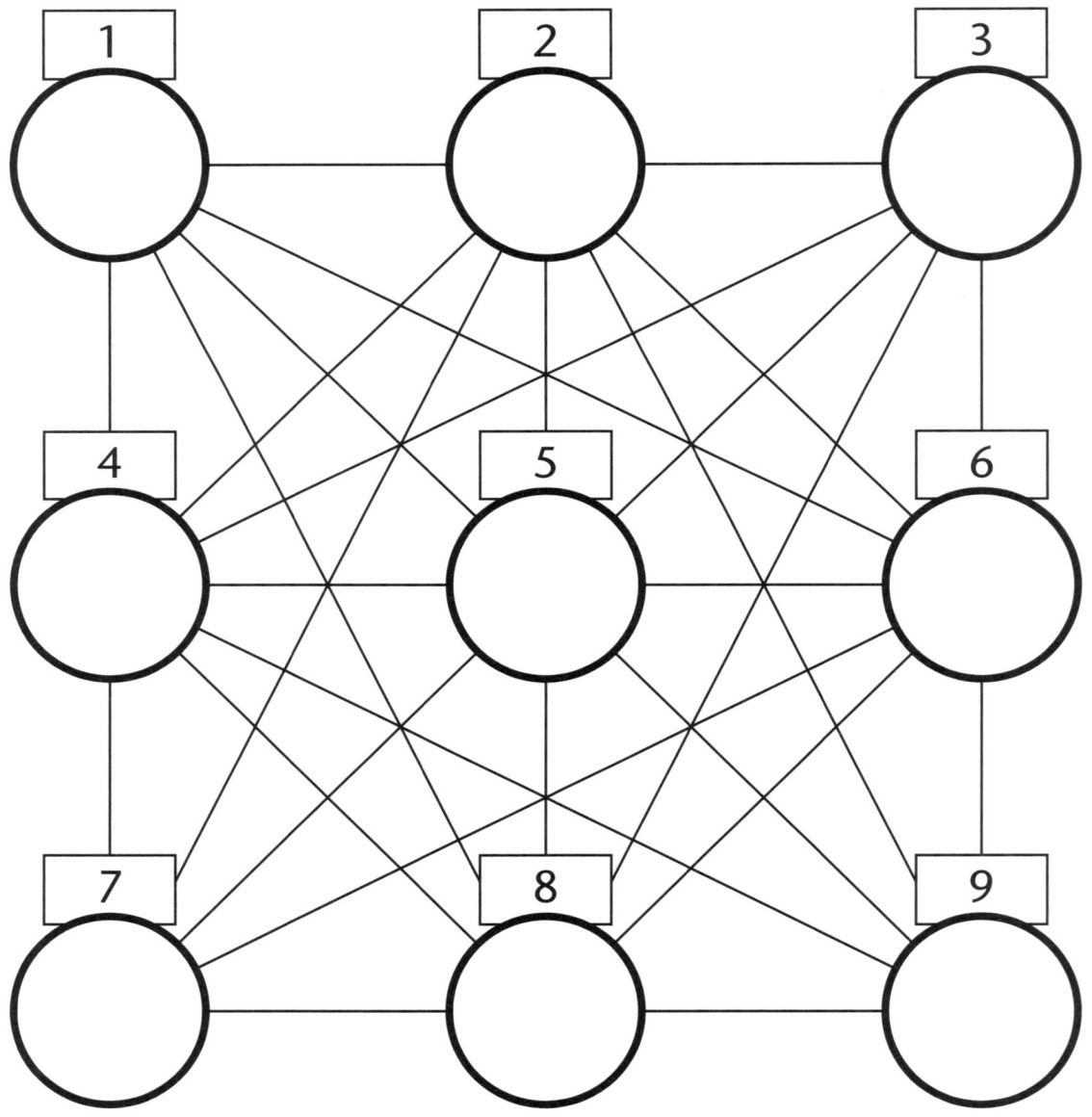

Name ....

Pick a path

Start in the square marked '**£1**' and imagine you have £1 to spend. Move to another square and subtract the number inside the square from your money. Move to another square and subtract again. Keep on doing this as you move towards the bottom row. You can move in any direction to a square next to your square. Try to reach a square on the Finish line with exactly that amount of money left. Find a path to reach each of the squares on the Finish line.

2p	5p	£1	8p	3p
9p	6p	9p	6p	3p
9p	5p	8p	7p	9p
8p	4p	7p	9p	6p

Finish line | 77p | 58p | 67p | 57p | 12p |

Plot some new routes on the grids below and write on the Finish line how much money you would have.

2p	5p	£1	8p	3p
9p	6p	9p	6p	3p
9p	5p	8p	7p	9p
8p	4p	7p	9p	6p

2p	5p	£1	8p	3p
9p	6p	9p	6p	3p
9p	5p	8p	7p	9p
8p	4p	7p	9p	6p

....

....

2p	5p	£1	8p	3p
9p	6p	9p	6p	3p
9p	5p	8p	7p	9p
8p	4p	7p	9p	6p

2p	5p	£1	8p	3p
9p	6p	9p	6p	3p
9p	5p	8p	7p	9p
8p	4p	7p	9p	6p

....

....

⑨ Using a pencil and paper procedure, or mentally, can subtract a 2-digit from a 2-digit number with no exchange

ACTIVITY 9.1

Resources
- none (an enlarged copy of the pictures below is optional)

♦ – ♠   ☆ – ✔

✈ – ▼   ♥ – ●

☆ – ♦   ✈ – ✔

♦ – ➡   etc.

A big difference?

On the board draw a grid like the one shown below.

♦	♥	♠	▼	☆	✏	✈	✂	✔	➡	♣	●
26	32	14	12	27	15	19	35	16	11	48	21

Ask the children to work out how much a star minus a pencil is worth. Show this operation as a subtraction question, that is, 27 – 15.

Choose other questions which involve no exchange, for example, those on the left.

For consolidation of this idea you can use Activity 9.2 *'Making a difference'* below.

ACTIVITY 9.2

Resources
- 'Making a difference' sheet on page 33

Making a difference

You can use this sheet to continue Activity 9.1 *'A big difference?'*. Children are required to solve subtraction questions, involving subtraction of 2-digit numbers without exchange. Encourage children to work mentally and discuss children's methods as a group.

ACTIVITY 9.3

Resources
- none

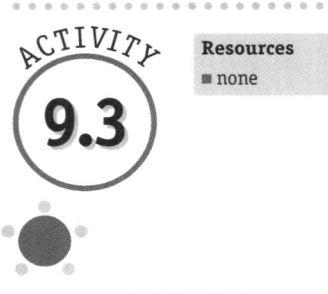

9 – ☐☐ = 2☐

Solving subtractions

This investigation can assist children to see that patterns repeat themselves as numbers are increased by ten, and also allows children the chance to explore subtraction as the inverse of addition.

Ask children, in groups, to explore all the possible solutions to the question on the left.

To begin with, it may be useful for children to take a different tens digit, for example, one child may take 99, another 89, another 79, etc.

How many possible answers give an answer in the 'twenties'?

Encourage the groups to present their information in a poster form and to systematically ensure that all solutions are found.

These are the patterns of the solutions.

99–79=20   99–78=21   99–77=22   99–76=23   99–75=24   up to 99–70=29

89–69=20   89–68=21   89–67=22   89–66=23   89–65=24…

79–59=20   79–58=21   79–57=22…
.
.
29–9 = 20…   etc.

There are 80 solutions that can be made using positive whole numbers.

You can adapt this investigation by giving the groups a particular 2-digit number to subtract or by changing the units digit so that the subtraction may require the crossing of a 'tens barrier'.

Name ....

Making a difference

How quickly can you answer these questions in your head?

◆	❤	♠	▼	☆	✏	✈	✂	✔	➡	♣	●
26	32	14	12	27	15	19	35	16	11	48	21

(1) ☆ − ✔ = ...

(2) ✈ − ✔ = ...

(3) ✈ − ▼ = ...

(4) ☆ − ◆ = ...

(5) ♠ − ➡ = ...

(6) ✂ − ➡ = ...

(7) ✂ − ▼ = ...

(8) ✔ − ▼ = ...

(9) ◆ − ✔ = ...

(10) ♣ − ✂ = ...

(11) ♣ − ✏ = ...

(12) ♣ − ♠ = ...

(13) ♣ − ✔ − ● = ...

(14) ◆ − ♠ − ▼ = ...

(15) ✂ − ● − ➡ = ...

(16) ☆ − ▼ − ✏ = ...

(17) ♣ − ● − ☆ = ...

(18) ♣ − ● − ➡ − ▼ = ...

(19) ♣ − ➡ − ▼ − ➡ = ...

(20) ✂ − ➡ − ▼ − ▼ = ...

Do any of these questions make the same answer?

Why do you think this is?

10 Using a pencil and paper procedure, or mentally, can subtract a 2-digit from a 2-digit number with exchange

ACTIVITY

10.1

Resources
■ none

Units spot

Write the following 2-digit numbers on the board, as shown.

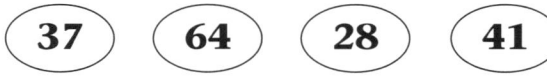

37   64   28   41

Explain that you are going to choose two of the numbers and find the difference. (Alternatively, you could say you are taking the smaller number from the larger number.)

Write this difference on the board, like this.

◯ – ◯ = 23

Which of the two numbers could it be? When children give the answer, ask them what they looked for.

Give some more differences, for example,

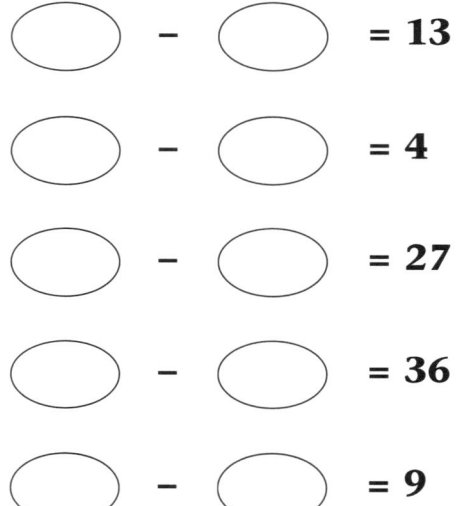

◯ – ◯ = 13

◯ – ◯ = 4

◯ – ◯ = 27

◯ – ◯ = 36

◯ – ◯ = 9

Encourage children to look at the units digits to find which numbers could possibly make the difference, then check the tens digits.

The activity can be repeated many times with different 2-digit numbers.

Resources
- resource sheet 2: star template on page 59

Stars in your eyes!

Draw a star with numbers at each point, in the centre of the board, as shown.

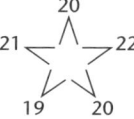

Note that these numbers should come within a range of 5.

Ask the children to come up to the board and write the difference between each of the numbers around the star, building a new layer around the outside. Continue to find the differences between neighbouring numbers, creating a large star pattern, like the one below.

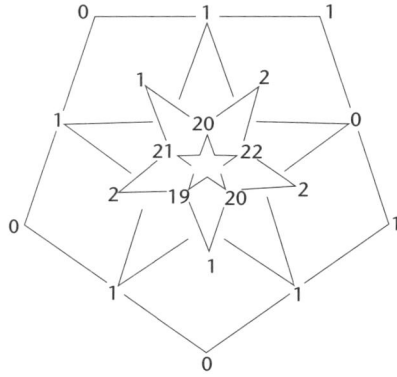

Eventually, the numbers around the edge of the star will begin to repeat themselves, with the majority being zeros. How many layers does the star have before there are three or more zeros? Choose some new numbers to begin a star, for example,

17, 18, 20, 21, 19

How many layers does this have, before all the differences are the same?

Find a set of numbers that never reach at least three zeros.

Children can continue this idea by investigating their own numbers and recording their work in their books or on resource sheet 2 on page 59.

Resources
- 'All change!' sheet on page 37

All change!

This sheet requires children to calculate the change given from £1 when different amounts of money are spent. Children may choose to solve the questions using a variety of methods, for example, counting back or counting on or using known addition facts. Children need to be able to calculate or recall the 'partners to 100', for example, 64 + 36, quickly.

Watch out for children who think that 64 and 46 make 100. This is because they have learnt that 60 + 40 = 100. Show them practically, using base 10 material, that one of the tens has been split into two parts, as shown on the left.

The second part of the activity, which can be done as a form of addition, is nevertheless valuable in assisting children to recognise partners to 100 to help with mental subtraction work.

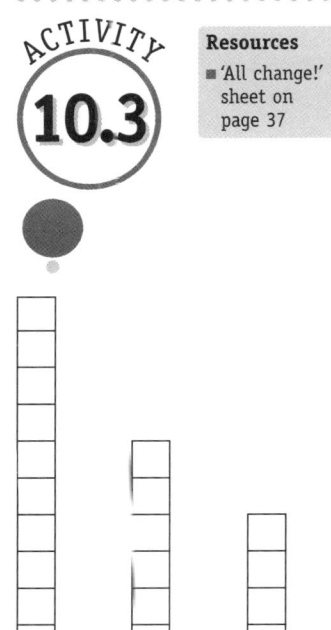

Resources
■ resource sheet 3: 0–9 cards on page 60

Making ten

This activity offers the opportunity to practise the subtraction of 2-digit numbers with exchange. Children, in pairs, alternately turn up two cards, giving a total of four per pair of players. Each player uses the cards to create a subtraction question that will give an answer as close to 10 as possible. If, for example, the cards 4, 1, 7, 3 were turned up, the players might choose to arrange the numbers in the following ways.

$$\begin{array}{cc} \text{player 1} & \begin{array}{r} 3\ 4 \\ -\ 1\ 7 \\ \hline 1\ 7 \end{array} \end{array} \quad \text{or} \quad \begin{array}{cc} \text{player 2} & \begin{array}{r} 4\ 1 \\ -\ 3\ 7 \\ \hline 4 \end{array} \end{array}$$

In this example player 2 would win the game by virtue of having an answer that is closer to 10.

You can introduce a scoring system whereby the winner of the round scores the difference between the two answers. In the example above, player 2 would score 13 points.

Target numbers other than 10 can be introduced for variety.

Resources
■ none

Switch the digits

You can introduce this investigation verbally or write instructions on the board. Ask children to follow these instructions.

Choose any 2-digit number and write it down.

Next, 'switch the digits', like this.

63   switch ...   36

$$\begin{array}{r} 6\ 3 \\ -\ 3\ 6 \\ \hline 2\ 7 \end{array}$$

Write the smaller number underneath the larger and subtract (or find the difference).

If your new number has two different digits, then begin this process again, for example, in this case 27 is switched to become 72 and subtracted, etc.

Continue this process until both the tens digit and the units digit is the same, or you have a single-digit number.

What do you notice? Try other numbers.

For all 2-digit numbers which have a different tens digit and units digit:

● it will always 'reduce' to become 9,

● the first subtraction will always produce a number in the 9 times table.

For 2-digit numbers with the same digits:

● the first subtraction will produce zero.

Name ....

All change!

You have been given £1 to spend. How much change would you be given if you bought the following items?

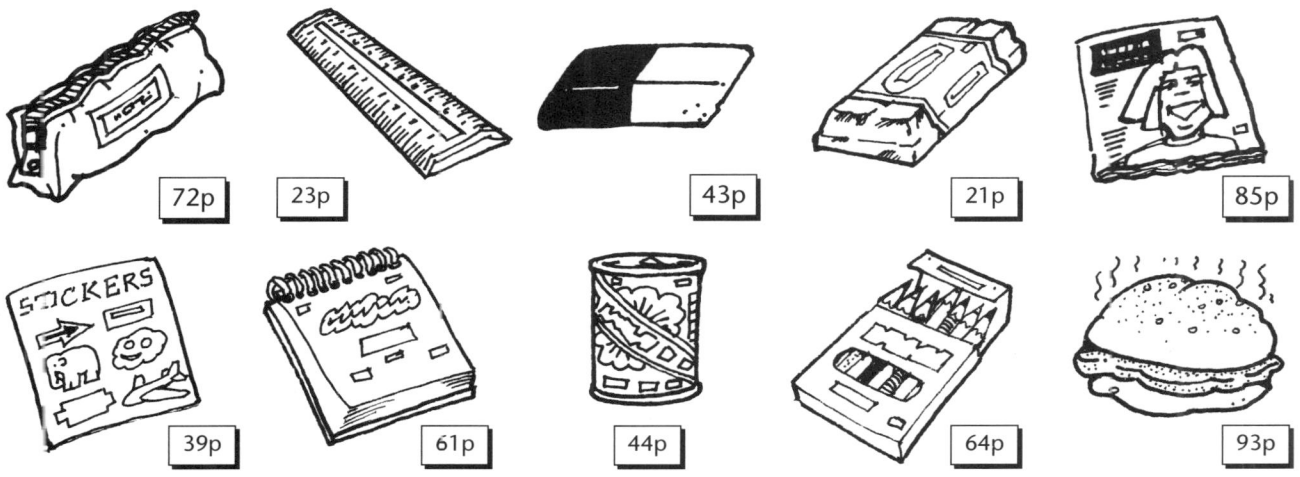

Fill in this table.

Money to spend	Price of item	Change
£1	72p	
£1	23p	
£1	43p	
£1	21p	
£1	85p	
£1	39p	
£1	61p	
£1	44p	
£1	64p	
£1	93p	

Look at the numbers below. Link up the numbers that make 100. One has been done for you already.

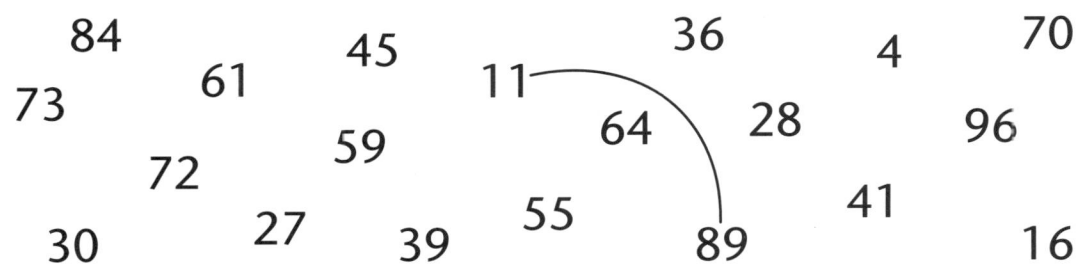

(11) Understands place value ideas to 1000

Further place value ideas can be found in the Place Value Teaching and Learning Activity Book *in this series.*

Resources
- none

One-step snake

Begin by drawing a snake, like the one on the left, on to a board or large piece of paper. You can write in the numbers shown or make up your own.

Ask the children, one at a time, to describe the step from one number to the next, for example, add 2, take away 100, add 20, and so on. For children who are experiencing difficulties, give them a calculator to check other children's answers.

10 12 22 122 102 100 90 98

Resources
- 'Finding your way' sheet on page 39

Finding your way

This sheet provides practice in identifying the components of numbers to 1000, for example, recognising that there are 7 tens in 276 and 370. Children are asked to colour numbers according to their parts. If completed correctly, a continuous path of red weaves from top to bottom.

Resources
- calculators

Disappearing digits

Ask children to key a 3-digit number into the calculator. They have to make each of the digits disappear, leaving an empty space or a zero. They must do this by subtracting the correct amount. If they have been introduced to the Superheroes idea in the *Place Value Teaching and Learning Activity Book* in this series, encourage the children to talk of this digit as 'I'm going to make Hundreds Woman disappear!'.

453 − 50 = 403

For example, if our number is 453, we must subtract 50 in order to remove the tens digit, as shown on the left.

This activity helps children to focus on the value of each digit as determined by its position in a number. At first, children may make mistakes, for example, to remove Tens Man in the number 453 children may subtract 5, rather than 50. If mistakes are made, ask them to try adding the number they subtracted to return to the original number.

Further explanation of the Superheroes can be found in unit 13 (pages 43–45) of this book.

Resources
- one calculator per child

Changing targets

A game for two players. Player 1 enters a 3-digit number into his calculator, for example, 547. Player 2 enters the same number into her calculator but with 1 digit changed, for example, 247, 517 or 546. Player 1 must change his display to match that of player 2 in one operation, as in subtracting 300 if the new number is 247. If player 1 is correct, he scores 1 point. Then player 2 selects a number and the game continues. The winner is the first player to score 11 points. This activity helps children to focus on the value of each digit as determined by its position in a number.

Name ....

Finding your way

The numbers on the right can be broken into parts.

For example,

267 is made up from 2 hundreds, 6 tens and 7 units.

Colour in the parts of these numbers using this key.

2 tens:	Red
7 hundreds:	Yellow
1 hundred:	Green
6 hundreds:	Red
0 tens:	Blue
5 units:	Yellow
8 units:	Red
2 units:	Blue
4 tens:	Green
3 hundreds:	Red
1 unit:	Yellow
5 tens:	Red
9 tens:	Green
8 tens:	Red
8 hundreds:	Blue
6 units:	Red
4 units:	Yellow
2 hundreds:	Green

H	T	U
3	5	8
6	9	4
3	2	2
2	5	1
7	8	6
8	0	8
6	2	6
3	4	5
6	5	2
1	2	4

⑫ Using a pencil and paper procedure, or mentally, can subtract a 2/3-digit from a 3-digit number with no exchange

ACTIVITY 12.1

Resources
- none

From right to left

On the board draw a table like the one shown below.

Hundreds	Tens	Units
5	4	6
− 3	1	2

Cover up the hundreds and tens columns and then ask the children to do the subtraction in the units column. Write the answer underneath and then move on to the tens column, covering the hundreds and units, and finally to the hundreds.

Discuss with the children the ease with which they worked out the answers for each column. Remind them that when they have a subtraction question on paper they need to remember to work from right to left, always starting with the units column.

Many children panic when they see sums with large numbers, and fail to break down each column into hundreds, tens and units. They therefore believe the sum is too difficult. Ensure that the children understand that the number can be 'partitioned' into hundreds, tens and units and dealt with one column at a time.

Encourage the children to estimate the answer to improve their 'sense' of what the answer might be.

ACTIVITY 12.2

Resources
- 'Line up' sheet on page 41
- counters or coloured pencils

Line up

This is a game for 2 players. The pair will need one 'Line up' sheet on page 41 between them. Each player, in turn, chooses a number from the top row. They then select, from the bottom row, a number to subtract from this number. If the answer is in the grid, a counter is placed on that number. If counters are not available, the squares can be shaded in with coloured pencils. The winner is the first player to cover ten squares.

ACTIVITY 12.3

Resources
- 'Going far?' sheet on page 42

Going far?

This activity offers a context in which to practise the subtraction of 3-digit numbers without exchange.

Line up

Take it in turns to choose a number from the top row. Then each select a number from the bottom row and subtract it from your first number.

If the answer is the same as a number in the grid, put a counter on it or shade it in with your coloured pencil. The winner is the first person to cover ten squares!

889	697	868	965	797	678

215	104	430	344	404	545

674	274	133	621	393
593	535	334	574	764
252	467	453	693	367
750	861	561	653	438
323	482	485	459	785

Name ....

Going far?

Meet Neil. He is a van driver for 'Hall's Haulage'.

This is his list of deliveries for next week, showing how many miles he has to drive.

Mon	Tue	Wed	Thur	Fri
537	482	397	568	476

Each day Neil stops for lunch. He writes down how far he has driven before lunch.

Mon	Tue	Wed	Thur	Fri
226	171	206	366	234

How much further does Neil have to drive after lunch on each day? Write your answers in the table below.

Mon	Tue	Wed	Thur	Fri

Now meet Dave. He works for another delivery firm called 'Harries Carries Anything'. He has a delivery list like Neil's.

Mon	Tue	Wed	Thur	Fri
582	337	643	736	498

When Dave stops for lunch he writes down how far he still has to drive.

Mon	Tue	Wed	Thur	Fri
261	123	512	325	200

Work out how far he has driven before lunch each day. Write your answers in the table below.

Mon	Tue	Wed	Thur	Fri

⑬ Using a pencil and paper procedure, or mentally, can subtract a 2/3-digit from a 3-digit number with exchange once

Resources
■ base 10 material

```
H T U
2 4 5
- 1 2 8
_____
```

```
H T U              H T U
2 4 5   becomes   2 3 ¹5
- 1 2 8           - 1 2 8
_____           _____
                        7
```

```
H T U              H T U
2 3 ¹5             2 3 ¹5
- 1 2 8           - 1 2 8
_____           _____
    1 7            1 1 7
```

Superheroes

Choose three children to be 'Hundreds Woman', 'Tens Man' and 'Units Woman', for example. These are the 'Superheroes'! Ask them to come to the front and stand in a line as on the left.

Explain to the children that they are going to help you to do a subtraction question with the base 10 material. Write the number 245 on the board. Ask each Superhero to collect his/her part of the number. In this example 'Units Woman' will pick up 5 unit cubes, 'Tens Man' will collect 4 ten sticks and 'Hundreds Woman' will take 2 hundred squares.

Explain that from the 245 we need to subtract 128. Write this on the board as on the left.

Approach 'Units Woman' and say you have to take 8 of her unit cubes. She only has 5, so what can she do? She must ask 'Tens Man' for help. 'Tens Man' exchanges one of his tens for 10 unit cubes and passes these to 'Units Woman'. Now you can take 8 from the 15 units she is holding. Write the answer to that part of the calculation in the units column, showing the decomposition that took place.

Now tell 'Tens Man' that you need to take 2 of his tens, which he gives you. Write this as part of the calculation.

Finally, explain to 'Hundreds Woman' that you need to take 1 of her hundred squares. Complete the written calculation.

Repeat the activity with other subtraction questions that require exchange once, including those which will require 'Tens Man' to ask 'Hundreds Woman' for help.

This activity can make the process of written subtraction with decomposition, as above, into a 'real' experience for children which, as a result, they are more likely to understand.

Resources
■ 'A different approach' sheet on page 44

A different approach

This activity offers the opportunity to practise the subtraction of 3-digit numbers with exchange once.

Resources
■ 'Letters play' sheet on page 45

Letters play

This activity offers the opportunity to practise the subtraction of 3-digit numbers with exchange once. Children are given a series of subtraction questions to solve and the answers are used to plot points on a grid. Two answers are given for each question, one of which is correct. If children have done the calculation correctly, they can see this readily as the points plotted should form the letter H. The incorrect answer given for each question is a response that would result from a typical subtraction error, for example, always taking the smaller digit from the larger regardless of position.

Name ....

A different approach

Ez, Jo and Sam are playing a special game of darts where they each throw five darts in every go. They are playing a game of 991. Work out new totals for all three of them by subtracting their scores after each go. The person with the lowest total after five goes wins.

	Ez		**Jo**		**Sam**
	991		991		991
score	136	score	252	score	153
new total		new total		new total	
score	217	score	164	score	109
new total		new total		new total	
score	153	score	182	score	248
new total		new total		new total	

Who is winning so far? ....

score	149	score	169	score	165
new total		new total		new total	
score	239	score	133	score	150
new total		new total		new total	

Who won? ....

931

| 480 | 519 | 617 | 860 | 127 | 351 | 771 | 703 |

Subtract each of the numbers in this list from 931. Find each answer in the grid below. The answers might be written across, up, down or diagonally.

4	3	1	4	7	2
1	6	0	5	3	2
2	8	2	9	8	8
3	1	6	0	7	0
9	5	3	1	1	2
2	4	7	9	8	2

Name ....

Letters play

Solve these subtraction questions. Lower down the page two possible answers are given for each question. Choose the correct one and use the co-ordinates given with that answer to make a shape on the grid.

(1)   3 4 2
   − 1 3 5

(4)   3 9 2
   − 2 0 4

(7)   7 5 3
   − 3 7 0

(10)   4 6 0
   − 2 0 5

(2)   5 3 7
   − 4 2 8

(5)   8 4 5
   − 6 8 3

(8)   3 5 0
   − 2 4 1

(11)   7 0 4
   − 1 4 4

(3)   6 1 4
   − 2 3 3

(6)   5 9 7
   − 4 0 8

(9)   3 0 2
   − 1 3 1

(12)   5 4 0
   − 4 5 0

Answers

(1) 207 (1, 6)   or   213 (4, 5)
(2) 111 (3, 5)   or   109 (2, 1)
(3) 481 (0, 4)   or   381 (2, 4)
(4) 198 (5, 2)   or   188 (4, 1)
(5) 162 (2, 3)   or   242 (4, 2)
(6) 189 (5, 6)   or   199 (3, 1)

(7) 383 (4, 3)   or   380 (6, 2)
(8) 111 (3, 6)   or   109 (1, 1)
(9) 171 (2, 6)   or   271 (0, 3)
(10) 265 (3, 3)   or   255 (5, 1)
(11) 560 (4, 4)   or   640 (2, 2)
(12) 110 (5, 3)   or   90 (4, 6)

Plot your answers on the grid. Remember (2, 3) means 2 across, 3 up.

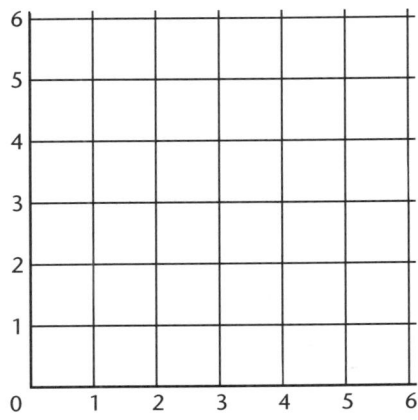

(14) Using a pencil and paper procedure, or mentally, can subtract a 2/3-digit from a 3-digit number with exchange twice

Resources
■ base 10 material

```
  H T U              H T U
  2 4 5   becomes    2 3 ¹5
- 1 6 8            - 1 6 8
                           7
```

```
  H T U              H T U
  1 ¹3 ¹5            1 ¹3 ¹5
- 1 6 8            - 1 6 8
    7 7                7 7
```

More help from the Superheroes

Choose three children to be 'Hundreds Woman', 'Tens Man' and 'Units Woman', for example. These are the 'Superheroes'! Ask them to come to the front and stand in a line as on the left.

Explain to the children that they are going to help you to do a subtraction question with the base 10 material. Write the number 245 on the board. Ask each Superhero to collect his/her part of the number. In this example 'Units Woman' will pick up 5 unit cubes, 'Tens Man' will collect 4 ten sticks and 'Hundreds Woman' will take 2 hundred squares. Explain that from the 245 we need to subtract 168. Write this on the board as on the left.

Approach 'Units Woman' and tell her you have to take 8 of her unit cubes. She has only 5, so what can she do? She must ask 'Tens Man' for help. 'Tens Man' exchanges one of his tens for 10 unit cubes and passes these to 'Units Woman'. Now you can take 8 from the 15 units she is holding. Write the answer to that part of the calculation in the units column, showing the decomposition that took place.

Now tell 'Tens Man' that you need to take 6 of his tens. He has only 3, so he must ask 'Hundreds Woman' for help. She exchanges one of her hundred squares for 10 tens, which she passes to 'Tens Man'. Now he can give you 6 tens. Write this as part of the calculation.

Finally, explain to 'Hundreds Woman' that you need to take one of her hundred squares. Complete the written calculation.

Resources
■ the 1–9 cards from a pack of playing cards (you may wish to add four '0' cards)

```
player 1      or      player 2
   4 7 9                 9 1 3
 - 3 7 1               - 7 7 4
   1 0 8                 1 3 9
```

Making a hundred

Children, in pairs, alternately turn up three cards, giving a total of six cards per pair of players. Each player uses the cards to create a subtraction question that will give an answer as close to 100 as possible. If, for example, the cards 4, 1, 7, 3, 9, 7 were turned up, the players might choose to arrange the numbers in the ways on the left. In this example player 1 would win the game by virtue of having an answer that is closer to 100.

You can introduce a scoring system whereby the winner of the round scores the difference between the two answers. In the example here, player 1 would score 31 points. You can introduce target numbers other than 100, for example, 500, for variety.

Resources
■ 'Game on!' sheet on page 47

Game on!

This activity offers the opportunity to practise the subtraction of 3-digit numbers with exchange twice, in the context of playing darts.

14 USING A PENCIL AND PAPER PROCEDURE, OR MENTALLY, CAN SUBTRACT
A 2/3-DIGIT FROM A 3-DIGIT NUMBER WITH EXCHANGE TWICE

14.3

Name ....

Game on!

Ez, Jo and Sam are playing another special game of darts where they each throw five darts in every go. This time they are playing a game of 901. Work out new totals for all of them by subtracting their scores after each throw. The person with the lowest total after five goes wins.

	Ez		**Jo**		**Sam**
	901		901		901
score	199	score	186	score	78
new total		new total		new total	
score	197	score	177	score	257
new total		new total		new total	
score	188	score	79	score	189
new total		new total		new total	

Who is winning so far? ....

score	129	score	184	score	199
new total		new total		new total	
score	99	score	197	score	99
new total		new total		new total	

Who won? ....

Here is a chance for you to play: Start on 901. Think of a score and subtract it from 901. Write your new total. Have five goes. You win if your last total is the same as the finish number. Good luck! Maximum score is 260 in any go.

	Game 1		**Game 2**		**Game 3**
	901		901		901
score		score		score	
new total		new total		new total	
score		score		score	
new total		new total		new total	
score		score		score	
new total		new total		new total	
score		score		score	
new total		new total		new total	
score		score		score	

finish on 76 **finish on 121** **finish on 62**

15 Can subtract larger numbers using a pencil and paper procedure

ACTIVITY
15.1

Resources
- base 10 material

Final call for the Superheroes

The Superheroes activities in units 13 and 14 (pages 43–47) can be extended to provide a model for the subtraction of larger numbers. 'Thousands Man' can be introduced to demonstrate that the process of written subtraction for H T U can be used for larger numbers also.

  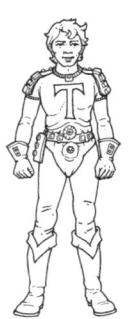 

ACTIVITY
15.2

Resources
- 'What a difference!' sheet on page 49

What a difference!

This activity gives the opportunity for the subtraction of 5-digit numbers. Children create their own 5-digit numbers and find the difference between them. They then investigate the nature of their answers towards finding answers that contain, for example, 5 different digits.

Finally, the children are asked to add the digits of their answers. They should discover that the digits of these numbers have a total of 9, 18, 27 or another of the numbers in the 9 times table. This is because when any digits are reversed and the difference is found, a multiple of 9 is produced.

ACTIVITY
15.3

Resources
- 'Tree fellers' sheet on page 50

Tree fellers

This activity creates contexts in which children can subtract with numbers beyond 10 000. The final part of the activity offers an opportunity to consider complementary addition as an alternative to subtraction, emphasising the inverse nature of addition and subtraction.

What a difference!

Write down any 5 digits like   **2 4 3 4 9**

Your digits can all be different or some can be the same, like this.   **9 8 8 4 2**

Write your 5 digits here. ....

Arrange your digits in different ways to find the:

   largest possible number ....

   smallest possible number ....

Find the difference between these two numbers. ....

Choose some different digits and do the same.

Try to find answers which match the list below. Write your answers in the correct spaces.

   all digits different ....

   2 digits the same ....

   3 digits the same ....

   4 digits the same ....

   all 5 digits the same ....

Add together all the digits in each of your answers,
for example, if your answer is 41976 then $4 + 1 + 9 + 7 + 6 = 27$.
Write down all your answers like this.
What do you notice about your answers? (Think about your times tables!)

....

....

....

....

Name ....

Tree fellers

Jeremy, Brian and Steve run a timber company. They deliver wood all over Europe in their 8 lorries. Read the milometers and work out how far each lorry has travelled on its last journey.

		lorry 1	**lorry 2**	**lorry 3**	**lorry 4**
Milometer	before	54542	34671	26482	76234
	after	54653	35624	27115	79103
	Answers:	....	....	....	....

		lorry 5	**lorry 6**	**lorry 7**	**lorry 8**
Milometer	before	33443	71849	63829	33856
	after	41126	88100	72000	40000
	Answers:	....	....	....	....

On their days off, Jeremy, Brian and Steve go to watch football matches whenever they can. Here are the attendance figures showing the number of people at each match they went to last season.

Manchester United v Spurs	55 281	Newcastle United v Chelsea	38 502
Blackburn Rovers v Aston Villa	37 200	Liverpool v Leeds United	43 627
Sheffield Wednesday v Arsenal	30 232	Derby County v West Ham	19 879

How many more people went to see:

Manchester United v Spurs **than** Newcastle United v Chelsea? ....

Blackburn Rovers v Aston Villa **than** Sheffield Wednesday v Arsenal? ....

Liverpool v Leeds United **than** Newcastle United v Chelsea? ....

Blackburn Rovers v Aston Villa **than** Derby County v West Ham? ....

Manchester United v Spurs **than** Sheffield Wednesday v Arsenal? ....

Newcastle United v Chelsea **than** Blackburn Rovers v Aston Villa? ....

Sheffield Wednesday v Arsenal **than** Derby County v West Ham? ....

Which two attendances have a difference of:

6427? ....

6968? ....

11 654? ....

25 049? ....

35 402? ....

16 Can subtract decimals

Further activities for the subtraction of decimals can be found in the Decimals Teaching and Learning Activity Book *in this series.*

ACTIVITY 16.1

Resources
■ none

Subtraction suns

Draw the following picture on the board.

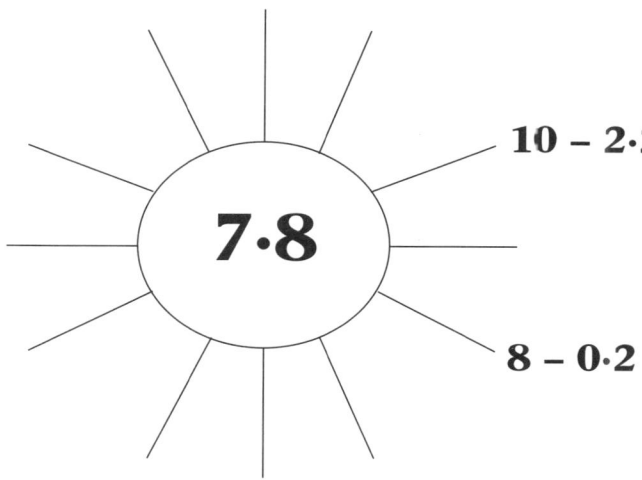

Ask children to suggest a subtraction question that would give the number inside the sun. Write this question at the end of one of the sun's rays. Children can do this as a whole-class, group or individual activity. They can use a calculator to check answers.

ACTIVITY 16.2

Resources
■ 'Reaching the target' sheet on page 52

Reaching the target

Children can work individually to find the number that must be subtracted from each decimal number to give the target answer. The later questions involve hundredths as well as tenths.

ACTIVITY 16.3

Resources
■ 'Formula 1' sheet on page 53

Formula 1

This activity gives the opportunity for children to try graded questions involving subtraction of decimals. The race track context provides a table of racers' times in seconds. Children are asked to work out by how many seconds one racer beat another. Questions for lap 1 involve subtraction without exchange, lap 2 requires exchange once, lap 3 exchange two and three times and lap 4 exchange up to three times with zeros.

Name ....

Reaching the target

What is the difference between each of these numbers and the target number below it?

8·0	10·0	5·5	7·6	8·2	5·8	12·5	10·4

Target   (**1·0**)   (**3·0**)   (**4·5**)   (**3·2**)   (**5·6**)   (**4·1**)   (**8·7**)   (**9·6**)

13·5	16·9	23·0	24·5	27·3	19·2	10·1	11·1

Target   (**10·0**)   (**11·6**)   (**5·7**)   (**14·6**)   (**20·1**)   (**12·6**)   (**8·7**)   (**9·2**)

Now try these.

16·7	12·0	34·6	45·2	30·1	50·7	30·0	40·0

Target   (**12·9**)   (**8·4**)   (**25·8**)   (**20·5**)   (**20·0**)   (**25·0**)   (**17·3**)   (**39·9**)

Try these with hundredths as well as tenths.

14·56	16·78	23·43	10·64	10·01

Target   (**10·00**)   (**12·34**)   (**20·50**)   (**9·85**)   (**9·02**)

KS2 Numeracy Pack © Letts Educational, 1998

Name ....

Formula 1

Andy, Sandy, Candy and Mandy are playing a racing car game. The table gives the cars' time in seconds for each lap.

	Lap 1	Lap 2	Lap 3	Lap 4
Andy	57·45	55·73	49·13	45·67
Sandy	57·59	52·64	42·36	46·10
Candy	58·37	47·32	44·25	54·00
Mandy	51·26	43·82	44·52	50·05

Lap 1
1 Who was quickest on lap 1? ....
2 Write the order in which the racers finished on lap 1. ....
....
3 How much quicker on lap 1 was Mandy than Candy? ....
4 How much quicker on lap 1 was Andy than Sandy? ....

Lap 2
1 Who was quickest on lap 2? ....
2 Write the order in which the racers finished on lap 2. ....
....
3 How much quicker on lap 2 was Mandy than Andy? ....
4 How much quicker on lap 2 was Candy than Sandy? ....

Lap 3
1 Who was quickest on lap 3? ....
2 Who came second, and how much slower were they? ....
....
3 How much quicker on lap 3 was Candy than Andy? ....
4 How much quicker than 60·00 seconds was Andy? ....

Lap 4
1 Who was quickest on lap 4? ....
2 Who came second, and how much slower were they? ....
....
3 How much quicker on lap 4 was Andy than Candy? ....
4 How much quicker than 60·00 seconds was Mandy? ....

Make up some more subtraction questions about Andy, Sandy, Candy and Mandy.

17 Can subtract negative numbers

ACTIVITY 17.1

Resources
- number lines from –10 to 10

It's getting colder!

Draw a number line from –10 to 10 like the one below.

Introduce this as a thermometer scale. Demonstrate how we can count along the scale to show temperature changes, for example, 'It was 4 degrees Celsius this morning and now it is 3 degrees warmer.'

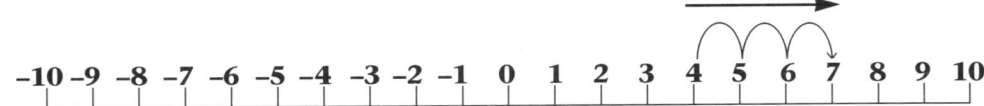

So we start at 4 and count on 3 to get 7, which we write as 4 + 3 = 7.

Show what happens when it gets colder, for example, 'It was 4 degrees Celsius this morning and now it is 3 degrees colder', by moving along the line in the opposite direction.

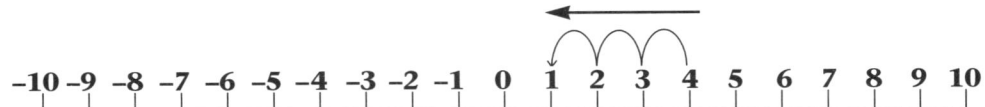

So we start at 4 and count back 3 to get 1, which we write as 4 – 3 = 1.

Show the effect of starting at zero and counting back 3, as in 'It was 0 degrees Celsius and now it is 3 degrees colder.' Ask, 'What happens if it is –1 and becomes 3 degrees colder?'. Show this and write it as –1 – 3 = –4. Ask children to come to the board to show other situations, for example, –2 – 4, –3 – 2, etc. Emphasise that numbers to the right on the negative scale are larger (have a higher temperature), so –9 is larger than –10.

ACTIVITY 17.2

Resources
- none

Going down?

On the board draw a ladder that is half below ground and half above ground. Label each rung as shown below. Ask 'If you are standing on rung 2 and climb down 1 rung, where are you now?'. Record this as 2 – 1 = 1. 'If you are standing on rung 2 and climb down 3 rungs, where are you now?'. Record this as 2 – 3 = –1. Ask the children to come to the board to do some climbing downwards from different starting positions, always recording the move as a subtraction question. The use of wallbars in the hall can make this a 'real' activity. Now pick a negative rung, for example, –1, and ask the children how many steps downwards they need to take to reach a particular lower rung, for example, –4. Write the question on the board, –1 – ? = –4, and ask the children to solve it. Discuss with the children how they worked out their answer.

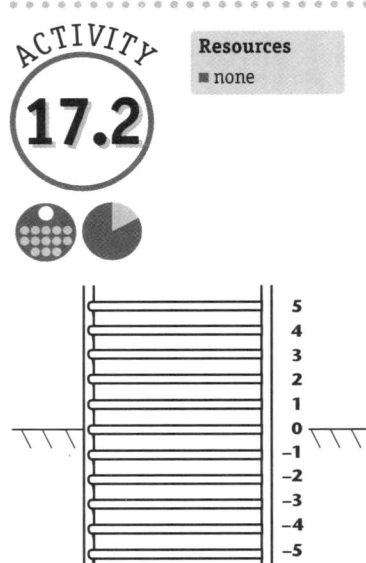

ACTIVITY 17.3

Resources
- 'Time travel' sheet on page 55
- calculators

Time travel

In these activities children are encouraged to explore moving up and down a number line which contains negative numbers, by means of a time-travel machine. The numbers correspond to years either side of the present, which is at zero. Further questions use the potential of the calculator to demonstrate how negative numbers are an extension of the number system children are already comfortable with.

Time travel

Here is a magic time-travel machine that can take us back in time or into the future. This year is at 0. We can go back in time (last year would be –1, the year before that –2 and so on) or into the future (next year would be 1, the year after that 2 and so on).

Unfortunately there is a fault in this machine and sometimes it goes completely out of control! It whizzes backwards and forwards, time after time, leaving passengers on board feeling quite sick and not knowing where they are! Where are we? The machine started at 0 and did these moves. In which year did it finish up?

(1) $-4 - 5 - 2 =$........

(2) $-6 + 12 - 5 + 14 - 20 + 22 =$ ....

(3) $-19 + 29 + 10 - 6 - 16 + 11 =$ ....

(4) $-1 - 5 - 3 - 6 + 5 + 6 =$ ....

(5) $-12 + 25 - 8 - 14 + 21 - 5 - 25 =$ ....

(6) $-8 + 10 - 12 + 4 - 13 + 39 =$ ....

Make up some more journeys for your friends to follow. Make sure you know where they end up.

Draw your own time line that goes from –50 to 50 (use a metre stick to help you). Make up some more journeys of your own using your time line.

⑱ Can subtract numbers requiring the exchange of numbers other than 10, such as time, Imperial measures...

ACTIVITY 18.1

Resources
- none

Tracks

Draw a simple picture of a CD in its case on the board, as shown.

1.	Moondance	4:30
2.	You wear it well	3:10
3.	Fool if you think it's over	5:59
4.	You don't know me	2:50
5.	Summertime	6:48
6.	Always look on the bright side of life	4:13

Write some names and lengths of tracks on the case.
Write the times of the tracks in minutes and seconds, and explain to the children that 5:59 means 5 minutes and 59 seconds.
'If the track was 1 second longer how long would it be?'

Ask children to answer a range of questions which involve them subtracting minutes and seconds, such as the following.
'If I had 10 minutes to listen to some music, which tracks could I play?'
'How long would be left if I listened to 'Summertime'?'
'How much time would be left if I had listened to 'Always look on the bright side of life' instead?'

ACTIVITY 18.2

Resources
- 'Board sailing' sheet on page 57

Board sailing

This activity gives the opportunity for children to try graded questions involving subtraction of minutes and seconds. The race context provides a table of racers' times in minutes and seconds. Children are asked to work out by how many minutes and seconds one racer beat another. Initial questions require no exchange of minutes for seconds. Later questions require children to realise that seconds are grouped and exchanged in groups of 60.

18   CAN SUBTRACT NUMBERS REQUIRING THE EXCHANGE OF NUMBERS
OTHER THAN 10, SUCH AS TIME, IMPERIAL MEASURES...

18.2

Name ....

Board sailing

Here are the results of three board sailing, or windsurfing, races held last summer in Cornwall. The time taken for each board to finish each of the races is given in minutes and seconds.

	Padstow	**Newquay**	**Penzance**
Sea Surfer	7 minutes 34 seconds	23 minutes 43 seconds	32 minutes 37 seconds
Sweet Sailor	6 minutes 13 seconds	21 minutes 23 seconds	35 minutes 12 seconds
Wave Walker	8 minutes 13 seconds	20 minutes 52 seconds	30 minutes 00 seconds
Tide Twister	9 minutes 25 seconds	22 minutes 15 seconds	32 minutes 01 seconds

Padstow race

1 Which board was quickest at Padstow? ....

2 Write the order in which the racers finished. ....

....

3 How much quicker was Sweet Sailor than Sea Surfer? ....

4 How much quicker was Wave Walker than Tide Twister? ....

Newquay race

1 Which board was quickest at Newquay? ....

2 Which board came second, and how much slower was it? ....

....

3 How much quicker was Tide Twister than Sea Surfer? ....

4 How much quicker than 60 minutes was Sweet Sailor? ....

Penzance race

1 Which board was quickest at Penzance? ....

2 Which board came second, and how much slower was it? ....

....

3 How much quicker was Sea Surfer than Sweet Sailor? ....

4 How much quicker than 60 minutes was Tide Twister? ....

Going loopy! cards

12	10	7	11
15 take away 5	14 minus 7	20 take 9	1 less than 20
19	4	16	8
the difference between 6 and 10	18 subtract 2	15 minus 7	subtract 7 from 10
3	2	14	9
19 take 17	take away 6 from 20	19 minus 10	3 less than 4
1	15	5	6
subtract 5 from 20	the difference between 8 and 3	12 minus 6	18 take 1
17	0	18	13
6 minus 6	2 less than 20	20 take 7	18 minus 6

Star template

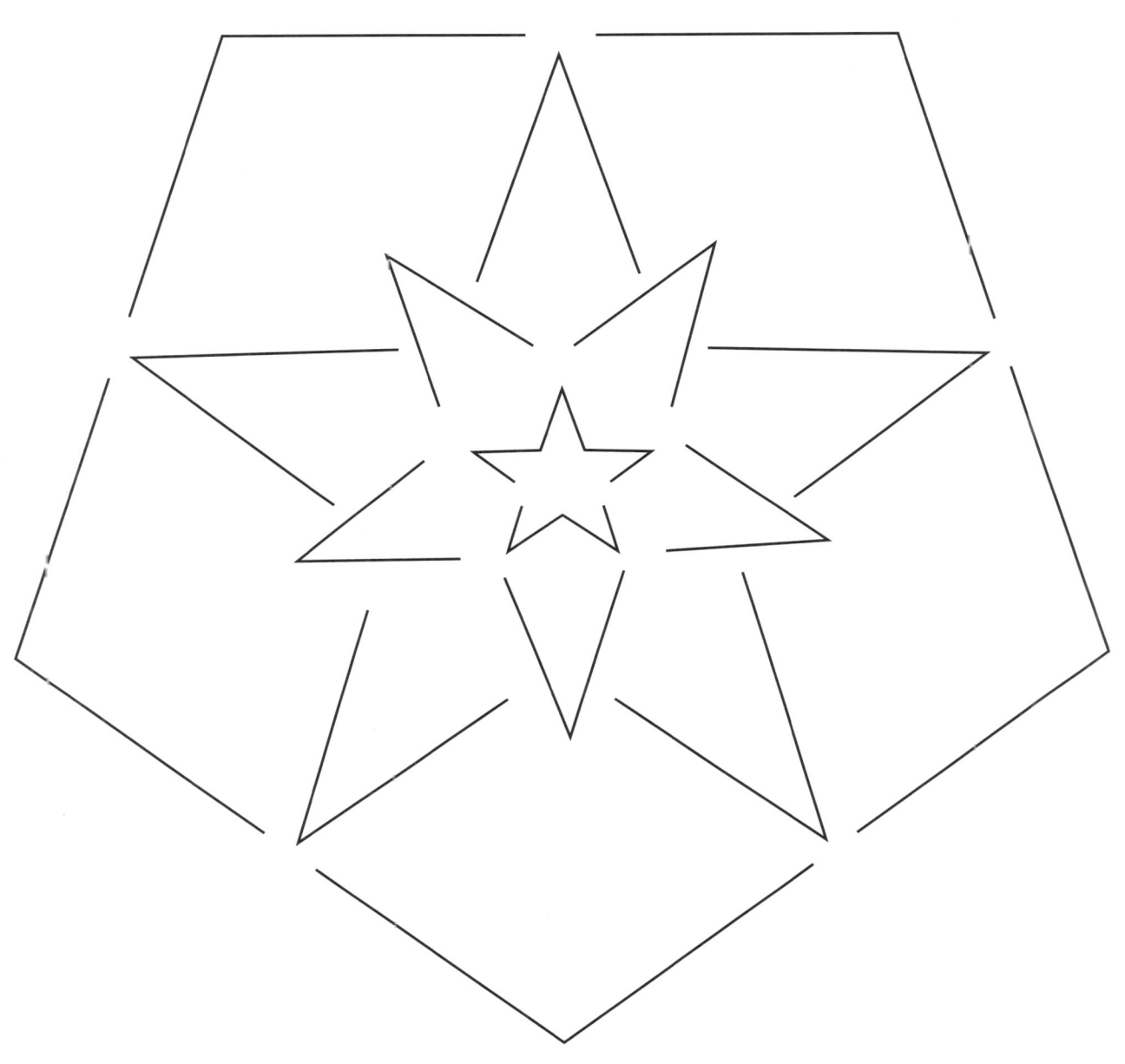

0–9 cards

1	2	3	4
5	6	7	8
9	0	1	2
3	4	5	6
7	8	9	0

KS2 Numeracy Pack © Letts Educational, 1998

0–100 number line

You can cut out these sections and stick them together to make number lines of different lengths: 0–20, 0–40, and so on to 0–100.

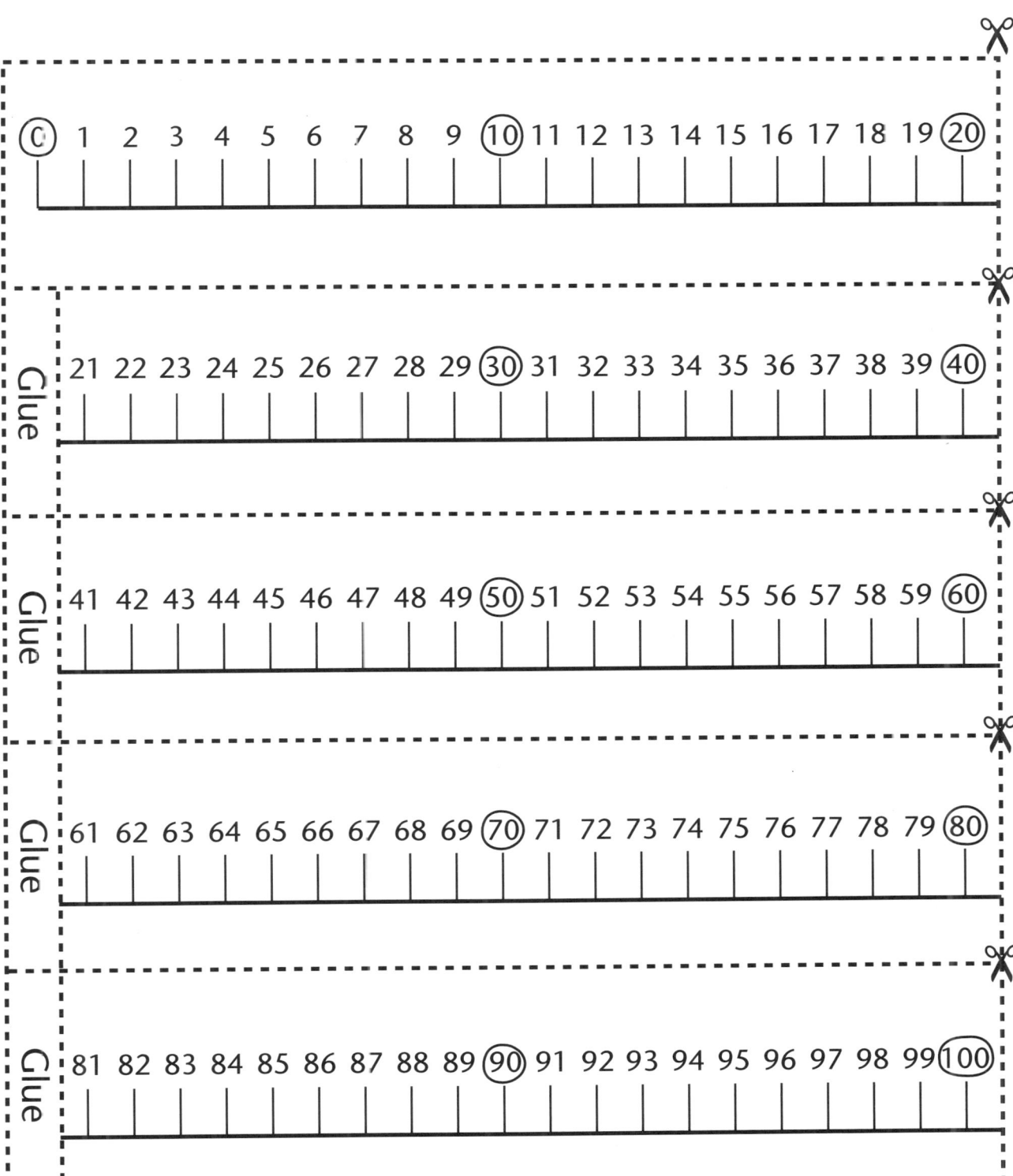

Addition and subtraction facts

0 + 1 = 1	0 + 2 = 2	0 + 3 = 3	0 + 4 = 4	0 + 5 = 5	0 + 6 = 6	0 + 7 = 7	0 + 8 = 8	0 + 9 = 9	0 + 10 = 10
1 + 1 = 2	1 + 2 = 3	1 + 3 = 4	1 + 4 = 5	1 + 5 = 6	1 + 6 = 7	1 + 7 = 8	1 + 8 = 9	1 + 9 = 10	1 + 10 = 11
2 + 1 = 3	2 + 2 = 4	2 + 3 = 5	2 + 4 = 6	2 + 5 = 7	2 + 6 = 8	2 + 7 = 9	2 + 8 = 10	2 + 9 = 11	2 + 10 = 12
3 + 1 = 4	3 + 2 = 5	3 + 3 = 6	3 + 4 = 7	3 + 5 = 8	3 + 6 = 9	3 + 7 = 10	3 + 8 = 11	3 + 9 = 12	3 + 10 = 13
4 + 1 = 5	4 + 2 = 6	4 + 3 = 7	4 + 4 = 8	4 + 5 = 9	4 + 6 = 10	4 + 7 = 11	4 + 8 = 12	4 + 9 = 13	4 + 10 = 14
5 + 1 = 6	5 + 2 = 7	5 + 3 = 8	5 + 4 = 9	5 + 5 = 10	5 + 6 = 11	5 + 7 = 12	5 + 8 = 13	5 + 9 = 14	5 + 10 = 15
6 + 1 = 7	6 + 2 = 8	6 + 3 = 9	6 + 4 = 10	6 + 5 = 11	6 + 6 = 12	6 + 7 = 13	6 + 8 = 14	6 + 9 = 15	6 + 10 = 16
7 + 1 = 8	7 + 2 = 9	7 + 3 = 10	7 + 4 = 11	7 + 5 = 12	7 + 6 = 13	7 + 7 = 14	7 + 8 = 15	7 + 9 = 16	7 + 10 = 17
8 + 1 = 9	8 + 2 = 10	8 + 3 = 11	8 + 4 = 12	8 + 5 = 13	8 + 6 = 14	8 + 7 = 15	8 + 8 = 16	8 + 9 = 17	8 + 10 = 18
9 + 1 = 10	9 + 2 = 11	9 + 3 = 12	9 + 4 = 13	9 + 5 = 14	9 + 6 = 15	9 + 7 = 16	9 + 8 = 17	9 + 9 = 18	9 + 10 = 19
10 + 1 = 11	10 + 2 = 12	10 + 3 = 13	10 + 4 = 14	10 + 5 = 15	10 + 6 = 16	10 + 7 = 17	10 + 8 = 18	10 + 9 = 19	10 + 10 = 20

11 − 1 = 10	12 − 2 = 10	13 − 3 = 10	14 − 4 = 10	15 − 5 = 10	16 − 6 = 10	17 − 7 = 10	18 − 8 = 10	19 − 9 = 10	20 − 10 = 10
10 − 1 = 9	11 − 2 = 9	12 − 3 = 9	13 − 4 = 9	14 − 5 = 9	15 − 6 = 9	16 − 7 = 9	17 − 8 = 9	18 − 9 = 9	19 − 10 = 9
9 − 1 = 8	10 − 2 = 8	11 − 3 = 8	12 − 4 = 8	13 − 5 = 8	14 − 6 = 8	15 − 7 = 8	16 − 8 = 8	17 − 9 = 8	18 − 10 = 8
8 − 1 = 7	9 − 2 = 7	10 − 3 = 7	11 − 4 = 7	12 − 5 = 7	13 − 6 = 7	14 − 7 = 7	15 − 8 = 7	16 − 9 = 7	17 − 10 = 7
7 − 1 = 6	8 − 2 = 6	9 − 3 = 6	10 − 4 = 6	11 − 5 = 6	12 − 6 = 6	13 − 7 = 6	14 − 8 = 6	15 − 9 = 6	16 − 10 = 6
6 − 1 = 5	7 − 2 = 5	8 − 3 = 5	9 − 4 = 5	10 − 5 = 5	11 − 6 = 5	12 − 7 = 5	13 − 8 = 5	14 − 9 = 5	15 − 10 = 5
5 − 1 = 4	6 − 2 = 4	7 − 3 = 4	8 − 4 = 4	9 − 5 = 4	10 − 6 = 4	11 − 7 = 4	12 − 8 = 4	13 − 9 = 4	14 − 10 = 4
4 − 1 = 3	5 − 2 = 3	6 − 3 = 3	7 − 4 = 3	8 − 5 = 3	9 − 6 = 3	10 − 7 = 3	11 − 8 = 3	12 − 9 = 3	13 − 10 = 3
3 − 1 = 2	4 − 2 = 2	5 − 3 = 2	6 − 4 = 2	7 − 5 = 2	8 − 6 = 2	9 − 7 = 2	10 − 8 = 2	11 − 9 = 2	12 − 10 = 2
2 − 1 = 1	3 − 2 = 1	4 − 3 = 1	5 − 4 = 1	6 − 5 = 1	7 − 6 = 1	8 − 7 = 1	9 − 8 = 1	10 − 9 = 1	11 − 10 = 1
1 − 1 = 0	2 − 2 = 0	3 − 3 = 0	4 − 4 = 0	5 − 5 = 0	6 − 6 = 0	7 − 7 = 0	8 − 8 = 0	9 − 9 = 0	10 − 10 = 0

Answers

PART I NUMBERS TO 20

(3) Understands that subtraction is the opposite of addition

3.6 Save, spend, save
Most, 5 Nov
Least, 9 Dec

(4) Understands subtraction as taking away and comparison and recognises when subtraction is necessary

4.3 Goal differences
Manchester United

PART II NUMBERS TO 100

(8) Can mentally subtract a 1-digit from a 2-digit number involving crossing a 'tens barrier'

8.4 Pick a path
77p=£1–6p–9p–8p   58p=£1–9p–6p–9p–9p–5p–4p   67p=£1–9p–8p–9p–7p
57p=£1–6p–3p–3p–7p–9p–6p–9p   12p=£1–8p–3p–3p–6p–9p–6p–9p–9p–5p–8p–7p–9p–6p

(9) Using a pencil and paper procedure, or mentally, can subtract a 2-digit from a 2-digit number with no exchange

9.2 Making a difference

① 11	⑤ 3	⑨ 10	⑬ 11	⑰ 0
② 3	⑥ 24	⑩ 13	⑭ 0	⑱ 4
③ 7	⑦ 23	⑪ 33	⑮ 3	⑲ 14
④ 1	⑧ 4	⑫ 34	⑯ 0	⑳ 0

Some questions produce the same answer because the difference between different numbers can be the same.

(10) Using a pencil and paper procedure, or mentally, can subtract a 2-digit from a 2-digit number with exchange

10.5 All change!

28p	77p	57p	79p	15p	61p	39p	56p	36p	7p		
84+16	45+55	36+64	4+96	70+30	73+27	11+89	28+72	61+39	59+41		

PART III NUMBERS TO 1000

(12) Using a pencil and paper procedure, or mentally, can subtract a 2/3-digit from a 3-digit number with no exchange

12.3 Going far?

Neil: Mon 311	Tue: 311	Wed: 191	Thur: 202	Fri: 242
Dave: Mon: 321	Tue: 214	Wed: 131	Thur: 411	Fri: 298

(13) Using a pencil and paper procedure, or mentally, can subtract a 2/3-digit from a 3-digit number with exchange once

13.2 A different approach

New totals for	Ez	Jo	Sam
	855	739	838
	638	575	729
	485	393	481
	336	224	316
	97	91	166

931–480=451   931–519=412   931–617=314   931–860=71
931–127=804   931–351=580   931–771=160   931–703=228

13.3 Letters play

207	188	383	255
109	162	109	560
381	189	171	90

(14) Using a pencil and paper procedure, or mentally, can subtract a 2/3-digit from a 3-digit number with exchange twice

14.3 Game on!

New totals for	Ez	Jo	Sam
	702	715	823
	505	538	566
	317	459	377
	188	275	178
	89	78	79

PART IV NUMBERS BEYOND 1000

(15) Can subtract larger numbers using a pencil and paper procedure

15.3 Tree fellers

111	953	633	2869	7683	16251	8171	6144

16 779
6968
5125
17 321
25 049
1302
10 353
Liverpool v Leeds and Blackburn Rovers v Aston Villa
Blackburn Rovers v Aston Villa and Sheffield Wednesday v Arsenal
Manchester United v Spurs and Liverpool v Leeds
Manchester United v Spurs and Sheffield Wednesday v Arsenal
Manchester United v Spurs and Derby v West Ham

PART V NUMBERS LESS THAN 1

(16) Can subtract decimals

16.2 Reaching the target

7·0	7·0	1·0	4·4	2·6	1·7	3·8	0·8
3·5	5·3	17·3	9·9	7·2	6·6	1·4	1·9
3·8	3·6	8·8	24·7	10·1	25·7	12·7	0·1
4·56	4·44	2·93	0·79	0·99			

16.3 Formula 1
Lap 1:　① Mandy　② Mandy, Andy, Sandy, Candy　③ 7·11　④ 0·14
Lap 2:　① Mandy　② Mandy, Candy, Sandy, Andy　③ 11·91　④ 5·32
Lap 3:　① Sandy　② Candy, 1·89　③ 4·88　④ 10·87
Lap 4:　① Andy　② Sandy, 0·43　③ 8·33　④ 9·95

(17) Can subtract negative numbers

17.3 Time travel

−11	17	9	−4	−18	20

PART VI NUMBERS REQUIRING THE EXCHANGE OF NUMBERS OTHER THAN 10

(18) Can subtract numbers requiring the exchange of numbers other than 10, such as time, Imperial measures . . .

18.2 Board sailing
Padstow:　① Sweet Sailor　② Sweet Sailor, Sea Surfer, Wave Walker, Tide Twister
③ 1 min 21 secs　④ 1 min 12 secs
Newquay:　① Wave Walker　② Sweet Sailor, 31 secs　③ 1 min 28 secs　④ 38 mins 37 secs
Penzance:　① Wave Walker　② Tide Twister, 2 mins 1 sec　③ 2 mins 35 secs　④ 27 mins 59 secs

 KS2 Numeracy Pack © Letts Educational, 1998